Beyond Psyche

aus
american
university
studies

Series VII
Theology and Religion

Vol. 239

PETER LANG
New York • Washington, D.C./Baltimore • Bern
Frankfurt am Main • Berlin • Brussels • Vienna • Oxford

Mark Gundry

Beyond Psyche

Symbol and Transcendence in C. G. Jung

PETER LANG
New York • Washington, D.C./Baltimore • Bern
Frankfurt am Main • Berlin • Brussels • Vienna • Oxford

Library of Congress Cataloging-in-Publication Data

Gundry, Mark R.
Beyond psyche: symbol and transcendence
in C. G. Jung / Mark Gundry.
p. cm. — (American university studies. VII, Theology and religion; v. 239)
Includes bibliographical references and index.
1. Jung, C. G. (Carl Gustav), 1875–1961.
2. Psychoanalysis and religion. 3. Symbolism (Psychology).
I. Title. II. Series: American university studies.
Series VII, Theology and religion; v. 239.
BF175.4.R44G86 150.19'54'092—dc22 2005016042
ISBN 0-8204-7867-9
ISSN 0740-0446

Bibliographic information published by **Die Deutsche Bibliothek**.
Die Deutsche Bibliothek lists this publication in the "Deutsche Nationalbibliografie"; detailed bibliographic data is available on the Internet at http://dnb.ddb.de/.

275 Seventh Avenue, 28th Floor, New York, NY 10001
www.peterlangusa.com

for NANCI
who saw me through

Contents

Acknowledgments

My heartfelt gratitude goes to all those who helped make this book possible: to Heidi Burns, Senior Editor of Peter Lang Publishing, whose welcome interest in my work came unexpectedly; to John McDargh, Associate Professor of Theology at Boston College, for initiating me into the mysteries of object relations theory; to Charles Hefling, Associate Professor of Theology at Boston College, for encouraging theological rigor; and to Lionel Corbett, Professor at Pacifica Graduate Institute, for embodying the religious spirit of the Jungian tradition with grace and intelligence. I would also like to thank Robert Gundry and Maria Amorso for their insightful comments and revisions, as well as family members Nanci, Lois, and Judy for their consistent support and encouragement, and finally my son Blake, whose earthiness helped retrieve me many times from excursions to realms beyond the psyche.

▪ CHAPTER ONE ▪

Introduction

My research into the topic of this book began in the following manner: when I started reading C.G. Jung, I found to my fascination that he pays close attention to the numinous symbols that appear in the dreams and visions of everyday people. I have since concluded that Jung's popular appeal must stem from his ability to stimulate similar feelings of fascination in individuals who like me find themselves for various reasons in need of a connection to the living symbol-forming activity of the soul. We can criticize Jung on many counts, as I will occasionally do, but let us give him credit for doing work that theologians should have taken up far more vigorously than for the most part they have done. A key question then arose in my mind: What did his attention to the symbolic level have to do with *theology*? What had Jung and other depth psychologists said that psychology could not account for through its own methods? In the end, I found somewhat to my surprise that an application of philosophical analysis to the symbolic function became necessary for an understanding of its capacity to communicate the emotional depth of the unconscious. Further, this analysis led to striking theological implications.

To the polemical opponents of Jung, his power to fascinate readers with tales of numinous symbolism signals that his work amounts to a Romanticist escape into the world of fantasy—an escape from the de-divinized modern world into a re-divinizing psychotherapeutic substitute for faith. Faced with the demise of traditional Western religions, these opponents argue, Jung used his creative powers to create a world of intrapsychic gods and goddesses that he intended as a cure for our neurotic disenchantment. It became clear to me that many of these opponents accuse Jung of creating his psychology in *bad faith*—offering a pseudo-religion, a helpful palliative for some, but not an authentic faith for the intelligent, honest modern person. I chose to begin Chapter 1 in the thick of such polemical arguments through analyzing an influential book by Philip Rieff, *The Triumph of the Therapeutic*.

I soon found myself disinterested in taking sides as a defender or an opponent of Jung in this battle but very interested in questions that my analysis of Rieff revealed. This analysis showed that Rieff failed to surmount the very weaknesses of which he accused Jungian psychology. He had nailed Jung for not coming clean about the post-Nietzschean demise of authentic faith in "sacred order" and had simultaneously heroized Freud as the prophet of authentic disenchantment. Yet he could not even state clearly where he himself stood in relation to the modern "hermeneuts of suspicion."

On discovering these underlying questions—typical modern quandaries over the place of truth in the life of faith—I wanted to find a path forward that affirmed a commitment to truth-seeking in the depth psychological study of symbol. And if I also wanted this path to go in a theologically viable direction, the commitment to truth had to avoid the foreclosure of divine transcendence brought about by the hermeneuts of suspicion. An article by Frederick Lawrence proved useful at this stage. He argued persuasively that radical skepticism utterly misunderstands the point of a post-Enlightenment hermeneutics such as Gadamer's. It fails to see the presence in human conversations of an immanent principle of self-transcendence—the "truth intention"—that orients the conversants beyond merely self-serving ends. Calling on Lawrence's work proved important again in the last chapter of the book, where I found that a similar principle of self-transcendence characterizes the symbolic function.

In order to flesh out the philosophical and theological issues that underlie Jung's work on the symbolic function, I needed in Chapter 2 to cover background material in the history of philosophy and psychiatry. The few critical, scholarly sources that extensively discuss philosophical influences on Jung made it clear that from early on he affirmed "the reality of the psyche"—an irreducible, immaterial factor essential to human life. This affirmation put him in the unenviable position of defending his "scientific" credentials while at the same time appearing to make "metaphysical" statements. He gained some support for his views by grounding himself in the tradition that historian Henri Ellenberger calls "dynamic psychiatry," including a strong tradition in French psychopathology, whose clinical and experimental studies gave evidence to the "discovery of the unconscious" and its subliminal levels of mental organization.

Having noted the debate whether Jung's "archetypes" and other theories measure up to scientific criteria or constitute a form of metaphysical idealism, in chapter 3 I turned towards the more elemental questions of how symbols form in the individual psyche in the first place, and how practically speaking we can understand symbolic activity as integral to the human subject's quest to live for the sake of goodness and truth. Several of Jung's early writings treated the symbolic function's operation in depth. By analyzing these early works, I found evidence that he was reading Asian religious texts quite extensively at the time and drew from this reading to establish his own view of "symbolic life," which he considered a correlate of meditative and contemplative practices.

I then turned in Chapter 4 to the question of whether I might use the correlation of symbolic to contemplative practice as grounds on which to argue that a transcendent presence operates in symbolic life whether or not Jung acknowledges it. First I had to pinpoint the effect of his philosophical subjectivism on the possibility that symbolic life includes a truly contemplative turn towards God. While Jung repeatedly denied that he ventured beyond the realm of psychic phenomena to the realm of things-in-themselves, particularly not to God-in-Himself, I never felt satisfied with this denial. Surely theology could come up with a more sophisticated notion of divine transcendence than one which envisions God as a supreme "thing-in-itself" standing cut off from the world.

Though his subjectivism effected a foreclosure of the contemplative turn on the level of theory, the actual practice of symbolic life as Jung describes it does not. When I analyzed the formal structure of symbol formation, I found that to function it required a differentiation of consciousness. Jung called this differentiation the "still point," but did not analyze it enough to discover that in understanding this still point lies the potential for a theology of divine presence in the symbolic process.

Selected readings from contemporary psychoanalysis supported the theological direction I was taking. Michael Eigen, for instance, developed Wilfred Bion's notion of "faith in truth" to illustrate the proper place of faith in psychoanalysis. When considered together with the differentiation of the "still point"—a self-transcending form of conscious presence—the self-transcending principle of "faith in truth" makes a theology of symbol formation possible. The creaturely transcendence of the still point and faith in truth leads to contemplation of their source in an uncreated transcendence that through them reveals its own reality to the soul. Of course, such contemplation requires a movement of faith, since it cannot demonstrate the existence of what it contemplates. Nevertheless, my analysis shows that understanding the formal structure of symbol formation in the human subject provides faith with an intelligible analogue to the transcendent presence which it contemplates.

·CHAPTER TWO·

Undermining the Hermeneutics of Suspicion

Jung has never lacked a bevy of critics standing at the ready to declare that he is not in fact an authentic psychologist at all, but a religionist of one sort or another—a mystic, a Gnostic, the guru-leader of a psychological cult, a heretic, and so forth. Given his sometimes cryptic prose and often esoteric choice of topics in the *Collected Works*, we can perhaps understand this accusation. Jung concerned himself with religious questions from the start; and he did not distinguish clearly enough between spiritual and psychological matters to please either theologians, fellow psychologists, or any number of critics from other disciplines. Through examining the arguments of one of his most incisive critics, Philip Rieff, I will analyze the most damning accusation against the religiousness of Jung's psychotherapeutic system. Rieff accuses Jung of bad faith. I will discuss the origins of the accusation, question its internal consistency, and finally propose a hermeneutic that puts an intention to truth at the heart of the "symbolic life" (Jung's term for a life engaged with the symbolic depth of the psyche).

In *The Triumph of the Therapeutic*, Rieff recounts the rise of "psychological man" and the character type of "the therapeutic" in the post-Christian world of the modern West. He wonders whether psychological man can create a new culture now that Christian civilization has died. The answer remains uncertain, because all known forms of civilization have in the past relied on religious symbolisms that human beings have taken as authoritative and psychological man rejects such "therapies of commitment." These symbolisms have provided socializing controls over our irrational instincts at the same time that they have allowed for the occasional remissive release from such strictures. "Civilized" culture successfully maintains a workable balance between control and release.

The strong Freudian influence in Rieff's view of culture comes across quite clearly. He pursues the purpose of his book from within the ranks of psychological men:

> Beyond its concern with the dynamics by which Christian culture has been displaced, the present volume will concentrate upon a struggle within the camp of one among these displacing systems of belief; I intend drawing certain implications for the reorganization of Western culture and personality from the divergence between Freud and those of his most powerful successor-critics studied in this book—C.G. Jung, Wilhelm Reich, and D.H. Lawrence.[1]

My analysis of Rieff's argument in *The Triumph of the Therapeutic* will proceed in several stages: (a) the historical emergence of psychological man, culminating in Freudian psychoanalysis; (b) the emergence of alternatives to Freud in the form of modern "religious therapies"; (c) Rieff's view of Jung's psychology as a "language of [bad] faith"; (d) an analysis of the questions underlying Rieff's argument; (e) an alternative hermeneutic that re-introduces the truth-question into conversations about depth psychology; and (f) a preliminary application of this hermeneutic to the questions raised so far. In the course of this chapter, it will become clear that Rieff, like many of Jung's critics and interpreters, fails to overcome the same philosophical problems that his discussion of Jung brings to light. After showing the reasons for this failure and suggesting an alternative approach, I will have reached the basic questions important for my second chapter regarding the philosophical and psychological influences on Jung. From this vantage point, in Chapter 3 I will turn to Jung's understanding of symbolic experience. Finally, I will move in Chapter 4 to the theological implications of this understanding. Chapter 1 ultimately proposes that we should not understand the relation of depth psychology to religion and theology through the lens of the "hermeneutics of suspicion" that my analysis of Rieff brings to light.

The Historical Emergence of Psychological Man

Although Rieff says that the nature of psychological man is still in the making, he recognizes a basic structure in this type. In therapeutic fashion, Rieff hopes to discern its implications for religion and culture; he makes us conscious of

---

[1] Philip Rieff, *The Triumph of the Therapeutic: Uses of Faith After Freud* (Chicago: University of Chicago Press, 1987), 2.

our modern psychological selves and our characteristic religious losses. Psychological man stands in the line of a Western development which moves from "political man" to "religious man," then to "economic man" and finally to the psychological type now in formation.[2] Rieff calls a member of this type a "therapeutic," or an "analytic" in the case of Freud. Political man lived the classical ideal of an existence inseparable from commitment to public life. Religious man represented the now-defunct Jewish and Christian traditions. He was committed to a sacred city and bound by authoritative structures that reigned until the Enlightenment. This type gave way to economic man, who called on the strength of a Calvinistic, worldly asceticism in this pursuit of "self-reliance and personal achievement."[3]

Rieff considers economic man the most short-lived of the types. It also differed from the first two by reason of its suspicion of commitment to a community, whether to the city of God or to the classical polis. These were replaced by the market, a neutral playing ground in which the acquisition of power and capital could take place without moral reservations. Therapeutic moral commitments were consigned to narrower spheres–to the family, for example. The transition from the economic to the current psychological type involved an even further narrowing. To the psychologically minded, the idea of a "neutral" market now appears more naïve than sinister. The neutrality of the economic playing ground is no more believable than the positivity of the old communities to which one committed one's life. We are no longer able to convince ourselves that social realities function through anything other than patently aggressive instincts. Sobered by his insight into the truth about communities, psychological man retreats even more radically from the outside world and puts his understanding of social bonds towards a more effective mastery of circumstances:

> In order to participate self-protectively in the manipulative and acquisitive game, psychological man builds his tight family island, living for the remainder of his time in negative communities. But these collections of little islands surrounded by therapeutic activities, without any pretense at a doctrine of salvation, are themselves infected by the negativity of the larger community and become manipulative arenas themselves, rather than oases of escape from the larger arena.[4]

---

[2] Philip Rieff, *Freud: The Mind of the Moralist*, 3rd ed. (Chicago: University of Chicago Press, 1979), 391. Please note that throughout this and the following two sections I will be speaking for Rieff's view, not my own.

[3] *Triumph*, 53.

[4] Ibid.

The family amounts to a social system as much as the market does, and power struggles and incestuous desires characterize it—not safety. Furthermore, the old controls which mitigated these struggles have not stayed in force.

Yet even the modern recluse finds no escape, since the soul too suffers conflict. Loss of faith in the world gives way to loss of faith in the confident Enlightenment self, so that his confidence turns into self-concern.[5] There, in the inwardness of this concern, he finds both the general affective chaos of the unconscious and the moralizing judgment of the superego. Having recognized the superego, the modern unbeliever discovers that "the great Father-God had never died."[6] The irony of this situation should not escape us. The very emergence of psychological man came about as an assault on the pretense of divine order. What Rieff calls "the vertical in authority" could no longer keep the self in the rightful place assigned it by religion, or even the semblances of its rightful place which persisted in varying degrees after the Enlightenment. Once the "Eternal I was exposed at least a century ago as the dummy acting for social order; and especially for the weakest in it," our age became "radically remissive."[7] This statement contains an unmistakable reference to Nietzsche and particularly his work *On the Genealogy of Morals*, which was first published in 1887, 100 years before Rieff made this comment in a 1987 preface to the 1966 book, *The Triumph of the Therapeutic*. Nietzsche ironically finished the Enlightenment's secularizing work by exposing the divine order of religious society as merely human, and the ruling Father-God as a projected fiction foisted on us by the resentment of the most pitiable members of the species. Yet without the divine vertical in authority, ultimately no grounds exist for accepting any vertical in authority—neither conscience nor duty nor any other false transcendent. According to Nietzsche, these vestiges of deity must also be let go.

Rieff's Freud is paradoxical. On the one hand, as a "moralist" he understands the value of repression for the sake of social order. On the other hand, he also wants to undo the neurotic damage that this repression has caused in some people.[8] Neurotics must free themselves inwardly from the tyranny of the Father-God by coming to know him as a mere "dummy acting for social order" at the same time that outwardly they continue to endure the stifling loss of instinct which civilized life requires. All communities by

[5] *Mind of the Moralist*, 390.

[6] Ibid., 370.

[7] *Triumph*, xii.

[8] Ibid., 377.

definition live in sickness to one degree or another, and psychological man should free himself inwardly from them. He makes himself aware of the sources for his neurotic suffering—the repressions and failed sublimations—without naïvely acting out instincts that could destroy his place in the outer world. He hopes that greater insight into the real sources of his suffering will soften its domination of his life. Having been brought under the dampening blanket of rational order, the irrational complexes will perhaps exist in a more workable balance with the adaptive requirements of life. All adaptations require some relationship to communities of others and some submission to the constraints of these relationships; but the Freudian analytic submits only outwardly, maintaining an inner freedom born from the knowledge that these constraints correspond to no eternal law. They are only more or less useful; and when their use for social order brings about neurosis in the individual, we may apply the technique of psychoanalysis.

In the consulting room, repression is the enemy. There we speak all. That is the only rule.[9] We ignore the usual controls of polite society. This release occurs privately, made possible by the personal distance of the largely unknown analyst. We come to know the Father-God as the moralizing superego, a necessary but often cruel ruler over the chaos of irrational dynamics lying beneath the surface of consciousness and expressed in the symptoms of ill patients. This God still lives in a psychic sense, but our knowledge of his actual non-existence gives us the freedom to relativize his intrapsychic rule for the sake of psychological man's goal—a sense of personal well-being. "Freed from all suspicions of divinity," we learn to be kinder to ourselves.[10]

If Rieff's Nietzsche prophesies on behalf of psychological man, his Freud technologizes, attuning the soul to its new-found nihilism. A post-Christian character ideal emerges in Freud—"normality"—yet not statistical normality, for most are abnormal and must strive to become normal. In the absence of a vertical in authority, self-overcoming steps in as a substitute for transcendence. We have suffered at the hands of our own natures, and the heroism of the Freudian analytic, such as it is, consists in overcoming our own nature, not for the sake of a god, but for the sake of the ego and its this-worldly satisfactions. "The aim of psychoanalysis is the aim of science—power."[11] Yet this humble ego, very aware of its own weaknesses, suffers disabuse from the inflated self-

[9] Ibid., 364.

[10] Ibid., 26-7, 55, 61.

[11] Ibid., 93.

image of the Enlightenment humanist. In an age with no believable transcendent consolations for life's unsatisfactoriness, modest hopes for reducing suffering replace utopian dreams of modern progress. The hospital, not the church, becomes the new "archetypal institution."[12]

Rieff calls the therapeutic a myth through which we hope to "assume command of the emotional chaos." It is "a response to the absent God," for "who, without Freud, would so well know how to live with no higher purpose than that of a durable sense of well-being? Freud has systematized our unbelief; his is the most inspiring anti-creed yet offered a post-religious culture."[13] He retains a "chastened" version of modern rationalism:

> Psychological man lives by the ideal of insight—practical, experimental insight leading to the mastery of his own personality. The psychological man has withdrawn into a world always at war, where the ego is an armed force capable of achieving armistices but not peace. The prophetic egoist of Western politics and Protestant Christianity who, through the model with which he provided us, also laid down the lines along which the world was to be transformed, has been replaced by the sage, intent upon the conquest of his inner life, and, at most, like Freud, laying down the lines along which those that follow him can salvage something of their own.... The West has attempted many successive transformations of the enemy, the world. It now chooses to move against its last enemy, the self, in an attempt to conquer it and assimilate it to the world as it is. For it is from the self that the troublesome, world-rejecting ideal of the religious man came forth.[14]

The instrumental rationality which modernity first turned outward against the world now turns inward, for the sake of self-conquest. Freud both destroyed the Enlightenment confidence in the human and affirmed its conviction that the human is all that there is.

The "Religious" Therapeutics

According to Rieff, the scientific therapy of Freud does not differ from the religious therapies of Jung, Reich, and Lawrence on the essential matter of the demise of all true therapies of commitment. The commitments of the pre-modern person derived from the vertical in authority, that same authority which Nietzsche and others exposed as a false God acting for social order. None of the therapeutics finds a way to bypass this assault on the sacred. In

[12] Ibid., 202, 260, 390.

[13] Ibid., 40.

[14] *Mind of the Moralist*, 391-2.

fact, it gave birth to them, and they embrace the dissolution of authoritative institutions for the sake of the only goal left—a personal sense of well-being. Yet this drives the therapeutics into an unexpected darkness that they cannot escape.[15] Having planned to free human beings from stifling social controls, they did not see the nihilism which follows their assault on the sacred.

At the heart of psychological man's failure lies the fact that he can tolerate and embrace all sacred symbols, but only so long as they do not bind him.[16] Can the sacred be sacred if it merely functions as one more tool for contentment? Rieff thinks not. This central question occupies his attention and comes to the fore when he moves from Freud and the analytic attitude to Jung, Reich, and Lawrence, who belong to the emerging type of the therapeutic as well. All four owe their existence to the demise of the vertical in authority, the therapies of commitment, and the heroic egoism of the Enlightenment. Jung, Reich, and Lawrence propose religious therapies to cure modern soul-sickness, but none of them believe in the old faiths any more than Freud did.[17] But even if they do not see the irony, they still propose faith. Only this faith merely simulates the old religiousness by which religious man committed himself to authorities which—among other things—judged his failings and weaknesses. Psychological man does the reverse. He commits himself only to feeling good and judges all authorities irrelevant.[18]

The religious therapeutics follow the Romanticist belief that the individual self has divine qualities that deserve release from society's constraints. The morally remissive tendency of and the modern collapse of transcendent moral controls thus conspire together, says Rieff. Religious therapies function as a kind of inspirational nihilism: religion is illusion, but if put to proper use and not taken too seriously, it promotes personal self-realization. Even Rieff suspects that this view holds some merit. He recognizes that faith can be a good cure.[19] What benefit can we expect the freedom which Freud's psychoanalysis offers to give us, he asks, if we are not striving for anything beyond the goal of a durable ego? Personal freedom may increase, but freedom *for what?*[20]

---

[15] *Triumph*, xiii.

[16] Ibid., 26-9.

[17] Ibid., 73, 76.

[18] Ibid., 46-7.

[19] Ibid., 90.

[20] Ibid., 93, 98, 109.

Rieff cannot countenance the fundamentally dishonest enterprise that he thinks the religious therapeutics engage in. They want the gods' blessings without having to obey divine ordinances. He puts his fundamental sympathies with Freud, but he does not relish Freud's pessimism. The rationalist pursuit of truth caused the loss of true faith, and Freud's "chastened" rationalism continues this pursuit. Commitment-less simulations of religion fail to accept the deconversion experience which Rieff considers normative for the modern Western person. In addition, he finds the religious therapeutics morally remissive. At least Freud sees the value of an outward commitment to morality for the sake of social order. He makes his nihilism conscious of morality's importance, for he knows the terrible consequences that would follow from a wholesale abandonment of public morality. The universe is indeed cold and without meaning, but the human loves that give it warmth deserve protection from our more destructive instincts.[21] Even though civilization claims a moral authority that it does not possess, we should not let this entice us to remissiveness, though Rieff believes the educated elite have largely fallen into moral dissolution.

Rieff on Jung's "Language of Faith"

According to Rieff, Jung, Reich, and Lawrence tried to sidestep the finality of the Western deconversion experience. I will examine his understanding of Jung in detail. He argues that Jung was deliberately seeking a new basis for culture itself. This basis revealed itself in a psychological inwardness through which one finds the eternal order that undergirds all religious experience.[22] Having known this archetypal structure firsthand, one may then move freely from any particular system of belief to another so as to adapt one's life to its own set of "dominant archetypes." The resultant spiritual eclecticism is thus open to all such systems but committed to none of them.[23] This religious radicalism goes hand in hand with a conservatism of social order. Jung's eclectic, religious unbelievers consist in a literary elite who depend on a stable outer world order so that they may go about their narcissistic pursuit of inner values in peace.

---

[21] Ibid., 138-9.

[22] Ibid., 88.

[23] Ibid., 97.

In Rieff's view, Jung identified himself as a prophet only at the end of his life in the autobiographical *Memories, Dreams, Reflections*. There he makes it quite clear that he developed his psychology not primarily through scientific inquiry, but as elaborations of a personal myth whose foundations had been laid in childhood. Jung's father—a Christian minister—struggled with his faith; and Carl Gustav witnessed the strain that maintaining Christian faith in the face of modern historical and philosophical critiques can cause. Yet even more significant to Rieff are formative experiences in Jung's early life, experiences that subverted religious authority. Several times the young boy came in contact with numinous revelations of positively un-churchly aspects of the living God. In one vivid dream, he descended underground into a sacred space and there came face to face with a great phallus on a throne. The adult Jung understood this chthonic deity as a compensatory counterpart to the overly pure and benevolent Jesus worshipped in his father's home. In another case, he became obsessively preoccupied with a terrible thought that was intent on entering his mind. When he finally let his guard down, a blasphemous image formed: God sitting on his throne in the heavens, dropping a giant "turd" on the Basel Cathedral.[24]

Rieff understands these visions as typical instances of Romantic rebelliousness, remissive releases from an overbearing divine Father who cramps the individual's creative self. Through these intense experiences Jung was freed from a dead Christianity and spared his father's sad fate. He took these releases as revelations and "traced the convergence of divinely inspired messages and scientific intellection into a religious psychology—that form of faith he considered best adapted for use in the twentieth century." The Christian religion was now failing in its therapeutic effect, and so Jung's life work was to provide a "functional equivalent."[25] In Rieff's words,

> There can be no doubt about the way in which Jung looked back on his entire life: his was a prophetic mission, viably designed for modern consumption as psychology. God had made Himself painfully understood to Jung; it was Jung's appointed burden, the purpose for which, as a small child, he had been accorded that dreadful experience of grace. It was his task now to communicate, through his matured psychology, not the God of the Bible or church but the dark, subterranean God of each man's secret life, who is unknown even to the holder of the secret unless he be informed of His existence by deep psychologizing.... Thus Jung found his way out of the religious impasse which had destroyed his father: in an integrative personal symbolism, in a meta-religion, revealed originally to himself alone, which he then translated, without

[24] Ibid., 110-13.

[25] Ibid., 109.

> disclosing its divine source, into a psychotherapy which could be useful in the revitalization of any and all religious contents. It is a meta-religion aiming at something beyond the criteria of true and false, or even good and evil. The ideal character type produced by it is neither mystic nor ascetic but therapeutic—a person assessing even his own myth in terms of how much it contributes to his sense of personal well-being.[26]

Utterly without criteria for truth or falsity, good or evil, Rieff's Jung is the quintessence of the therapeutic type.

Apart from his aristocratic conservatism, says Rieff, Jung follows the other Romanticist therapeutics in many respects, especially in the attack on rationality. The modern cults of Reason and Technology have disenchanted the world; and the Romantics lash out against this loss, though they have no reasonable counter-arguments against modernism. Jung often referred to himself as an empiricist who was only hypothesizing on the basis of the psychological data at hand. By this intellectual sleight of hand, according to Rieff, Jung intended to legitimize a psychology which at its heart amounts to an unfolding of his own personal myth. Jung, Reich, and Lawrence share an animosity toward science, rationality, and modernity.[27] They all agree with Nietzsche "that only an illusory history, or an illusory religion, or illusory politics, could lead human beings to a therapy of commitment."[28] Their response to the disenchantment of the world is thus to churn out new illusions that are designed to be therapeutically efficacious for the modern person in search of well-being.

Jung claims to have maintained a balance between the rational and the irrational. He had discovered a synthesizing capacity whereby reason and the energy of the unconscious fuse in the creative person and thereby culminate in action. This synthesis occurs through what he calls fantasy—a form of creative thinking which elicits a solution to the opposites of intellect and feeling. Rieff sees a background of misguided Romanticism in this theory:

> The Romantic philosophers loved dialectic with the Platonic teacher lifted clean out of the method. It became a neat historical trick, easily perpetrated: first one term, then its opposite, then—from behind one's back, out of the "collective unconscious"—the third concept, the savior, as a synthesis. No longer did the pedagogic interplay, the clash of reasons in a debate, justify either the method or the result; rather, the method was transferred to the stage of historical action, with that third term waiting all the time in the wings to come out and save the show. The clash of reasons became

[26] Ibid., 113-4.
[27] Ibid., 114-5.
[28] Ibid., 120.

> a story line, a mythic content, an attempt to keep the suffering audience from becoming restless while waiting for the entrance of the savior, who, when he does appear, never quite succeeds in gaining their attention. In the Jungian dialectic, that ignored savior is the Unconscious itself, in one personification or another, come to correct the intellectual arrogance of consciousness.[29]

The collective unconscious functions as a simulated eternity, containing a range of archetypal images which vary by place and time yet in themselves exist outside time. Rieff rejects Jung's synthesis as "no synthesis at all"; rather, it represents the anemic attack on rationality perpetrated by the disenchanted literary humanist who cannot properly mourn the death of a world infused with divine meanings. This humanist seeks solace in an individualized myth created through the development of the fantasies which arise from the unconscious.[30]

In short, Rieff considers Jung's psychology a flight from reality. It does not base itself on generally available data and admits of no scientific tests. The compendious volumes of his writing follow in the tradition of Protestant erudition, the supposed data consisting of nothing more than illustrations on an already-revealed system. His work also mimics the peculiar style of this tradition: "unreadability itself." Yet unlike the Protestant erudites, Jung's revelations cannot make any claims to truth, since they are of the post-Nietzschean therapeutic type. Even if the spinning forth of Jungian symbolism has a therapeutic effect on the fantasizer, for Rieff it is essentially anti-social and guilty of narcissistic indulgence. Subverting the scientific quest for knowledge separates one from the real world, which like it or not has lost the presence of the divine and numinous. We may only understand this world according to the cultural paradigm of science; otherwise, we have retreated into the consolation of private fantasies. Because of the ill-repute of any religion in modernity, Jung acted in bad faith and pitched his religion as scientific psychology. As Rieff says, "God-making, nowadays, is no small miracle."[31]

Rieff's Jung might counter that modern culture has its own set of illusions, one that is particularly unhealthy and that we are free to opt for another set.

> For Jung, the illusions enforced by the modern rationalist culture were no more operative than the rationalism grafted onto the old religious culture; they were

---

[29] Ibid., 116.

[30] Ibid., 129, 119.

[31] Ibid., 126, 114.

> threadbare, like a manual of administrative procedures. Instead, Jung thought the deeper sources of illusion were primordial and creative, unconscious though not rationalizing, and mainly anti-moral, remissive rather than controlling.[32]

We have another option, thinks Rieff. All therapies of commitment may depend on illusory histories, religions, or politics; but the honest therapeutic takes the analytic rather than the religious turn. Following Freud, he relies on no illusions at all, disenchanted with enchantment itself. "Freud came to disabuse mankind; to lift from men the eagerly assumed burdens of their 'erotic illusions' is to render inoperative all the classical therapies."[33]

Having been freed, psychological man can then embrace his nihilism with eyes wide open. He has no commitments, public or private. The simulated commitments of religious therapeutics function no better today than would the old, discredited religions. In fact, they make us neurotic because they encourage escapism. Our civilization has undergone an undeniable change. It has created a situation where "the alternative to neurosis is disenchantment, but not some deliberately cultivated and controlled enchantment."[34] We ourselves have accomplished the de-divinizing of the world through our scientific and technological mastery and must own up to this feat in order to claim our new maturity.

Rieff credits Jung for putting up a courageous fight against nihilism but thinks that Freud's acceptance shows even more courage. Moreover, the fight was lost, since Jung did not even perceive the nihilism at the core of his own religious psychology. Other than the passions as the one and only way of warming up the universe, Freud offered no alternative to the inheritance of nihilism. Jung was not so honest. He imagined that a renewal of the human imagination could counter the nihilist position, when in fact such a hope, even if achieved, would not overcome the fact that we live in a universe where human values are irrelevant.[35] Rieff ends his critique by offering a lesson that we can learn from Jung's failure: "Symbols of psychological analysis, if they are intellectually compelling, become what they must be wherever analysis develops fully into therapy: a language of faith."[36] I cannot say for sure what he means by this suggestive remark. Is he commending straightforward religious faith to us as the only true bridge from nihilism to salvation? Yet clearly Rieff

---

[32] Ibid., 121.

[33] Ibid., 120.

[34] Ibid., 137.

[35] Ibid., 138-9.

[36] Ibid., 140.

considers the deconversion experience necessary for anyone unwilling to sacrifice intelligence.

Rieff and the Hermeneutics of Suspicion

So goes Rieff's exposé. By his own admission, *The Triumph of the Therapeutic* is a prophetic book.[37] Though he claims not to know what the emergence of the therapeutic type will mean for the world, he explores the possible implications and employs an eloquent rhetoric of critique, all the while demonstrating his own inability to overcome the type's shortcomings. The book's strength lies in the rhetorical force with which it exposes a darkness in the supposedly liberating ideologies of psychological man. It reveals despair at the heart of modern techniques of contentment. Rieff persuades by appealing to affect rather than evidence. In the case of Jung, he has severely skewed the evidence and presented us with a Jung who only bears partial resemblance to the man we see in the *Collected Works*. Nevertheless, Rieff's prophetic insight has brought to our attention critical questions which Jung never answered adequately. To these I now turn.

When reading *The Triumph of the Therapeutic*, one meets two pairs of terms around which its theoretical problems revolve. The first pair goes straight to the nature of theory itself. According to Rieff, we must understand theory either in terms of *order* or of *power*. Pre-modern thought considered the act of theorizing as a participation in divine, transcendent order. This divine order established the "hegemony" of "what ought to be" over what in fact is. We must conform our lives to this ought. Modern thought considers the act of theorizing an act of power in which we use reason as an instrument with which to mitigate the sufferings of life by transforming the world. Instead of trying to conform to an illusory divine order, we use science and technology to increase our freedom of choice for the merely earthly options available to us.[38] As best we can, we conform the world to our needs and desires.

These "theories of power" came about "both as a response to the death of the gods and also as a weapon for killing off those surviving, somehow, in our moral unconscious and cultural conscience." Freud's psychoanalytic thought belongs to this type of theory. So does Jung's at bottom, though he pretended

[37] Ibid., ix.

[38] Ibid., 85-7.

to discover an eternal order within the structure of the psyche itself.[39] We might ask which type of theory Rieff adheres to. We have several indirect clues. He heroizes Freud's disenchantment and considers the destruction of divine order normative. He confirms this view when in the 1987 preface he states, "So I have satisfied the singular desire to say my own ironic goodnight to sacred order." Yet the next sentences may cause us confusion:

> I have aimed to take no sides in the permanent culture class wars between insider-winners, who believe in nothing sacred, and outsider-losers, who abide in an order that is nothing if it is not sacred. More precisely, I have aimed to take both sides, and ask no vexing questions in the older ladder languages of the faith that was and is the question in these wars.[40]

But the vexing questions unfortunately lie at the heart of his own thesis. If he cannot or will not ask them with regard to his own work, then he cannot discuss cogently their relevance to the therapeutic type.

To make clear what I mean, I must bring up the second pair of terms essential to understanding Rieff: *fact* and *value*. The opposition between statements of quantifiable, verifiable fact and the value-judgments of moral and religious discourse is well-established in the social sciences. In his methodological attempt not to side, or to side with both the classically and the therapeutically minded, he implicitly accepts the opposition of fact and value as a real opposition and as a necessity for pursuing his task of presenting the therapeutic type to his readers. He feels bound not to let values skew his discussion of the therapeutic type and the modern religious crisis. Presumably, not excluding what one values from what one tries to discover would threaten scientific objectivity. In this case, Rieff feels bound to say his goodnight to sacred order.

From this vantage point Rieff appears to be engaging in a discourse of power since he refuses to side with one or the other, the ancient or the modern, theories of order or theories of power; holds to the modern division of fact and value; and implies that value judgments simply project an imaginary order onto a valueless world of facts. Consider the way he describes theorists of order: They advocate the "hegemony" of an ideal realm over the realm of facts; that is, they believe in an ideal world, "a vertical in authority," and this faith exerts power over the world of facts by imaginatively binding it to moral obligations. This essentially modern understanding of order

[39] Ibid., 86-8.

[40] Ibid., xiii.

understands its importance as the *power* of the "Eternal" (values) over the "real" world (facts).

Yet Rieff contradicts himself, since his commitment to the facts, even at the expense of what he values, implies a commitment to truth worthy of any pre-modern theorist of order. I sense the shadow of at least one god left in his otherwise vacant pantheon—the god an Augustine would have named the divine Word, manifesting itself in devotion to the truth. Such devotion requires a very important judgment of value, the value of truth even at the expense of human happiness. Rieff is straddling a fence. Devotion to the truth drives him to unmask the power dynamics behind the religious therapeutics' attempt to reinstate "therapies of commitment." For this reason, he cannot come forward to the reader as himself a theorist of power. On the other hand, he appears cognizant that the "vexing questions" underlying his project are theological questions, which he wants to avoid. Religious values are essentially irrational, believes Rieff, and unopen to inquiry except through the faith commitments which modernity has discredited.

Given Rieff's dilemma, we should not feel surprised that when he does speak explicitly about the division of fact and value, the central theoretical problems with his book come to the surface and his explanation flounders:

> With rare exceptions, they [the scientists] still accept the Ritschlian distinction between statements of fact and judgments of value. They make fact statements; the task of making value judgments belongs to other specialists.... Notice the context within which Albrecht Ritschl, following Kant, had made his famous distinction. In Ritschlian theory, value judgments can only be made in reference to a communal perspective. According to Ritschl, Christian perceptions make sense only within the framework of a historic Christian community.[41]

The scientist takes leave of all moral commitments other than those inherent in the goal of science: the "transformative endeavor directed against the natural world." Rieff understands natural science as at heart a technological will to power over nature; he neglects the desire for understanding which also drives scientific inquiry. We also know that for Rieff social science uses reason instrumentally to manipulate culture and that psychotherapy directs this manipulation against the psyche.

What then of his own book? Perhaps we should interpret it as an act of power, a prophetic word intended to manipulate a culture in decline through the development of a compelling myth of therapeutic man. Yet he paints a dismal picture of the therapeutic, not a compelling one. Clearly, he feels

---

[41] Ibid., 256.

deeply ambivalent and cannot see his way out. He accepts the disjunction between statements of fact and judgments of value while at the same time realizing with chastened rationalists such as Freud, that the very tools used to dismantle the therapies of commitment themselves derive from the therapies of commitment.[42] In the language of fact and value, commitment to knowing the truth bases itself on a "value judgment" that the truth is a good thing to know. Rieff's confusion becomes quite apparent when he tries unsuccessfully to outline the difference between a scientific therapy (Freud) and an unscientific therapy (Jung, Reich, Lawrence):

> Now, two therapies may oppose each other, one claiming to be more scientific, but the scientific therapy arises less from within the Unconscious than does the unscientific one. Of course, Reality Principle notwithstanding, the *esse* of the external world remains its *percepi*. But the critical difference between religious and scientific therapies is in the locus of control and in the criterion of assessment. In religious therapies, the sense of well-being is measured against the commitment, which is said to "transcend" it. In scientific therapies, the commitment is measured against the sense of well-being, which is said to be "immanent" in the commitment.[43]

Thus the two differ only in appearance and degree. Even the scientific therapist grounds his enterprise in the irrational unconscious, though less so than does the religious therapist. What "less so" could possibly mean is unclear despite the cryptically idealist statement that *esse* equals *percepi*. Yet clearly the scientific therapeutic cannot escape the judgments of value inherent in his enterprise. In this case, he cannot escape the judgment that the ego's sense of well-being is the goal, the *telos*, which is worthwhile pursuing in the course of one's life.

Here we presumably reach the end point of our ability to speak rationally in Rieff's view; for the well-being of the ego is the myth of our age. We cannot transcend it. It is our own "language of faith." He feels ambivalent because two opposites conflict in his thought. On the one hand, we can level critiques in the style of Nietzsche even against science, which has essentially unconscious, irrational values at its base. On the other hand, Rieff wants but fails to show that science must somehow be different. He wants but fails to show that the analytic attitude must somehow have transcended the older therapies of commitment by its ability to disenchant through rationalizing the unconscious. "The language of science is not revelatory but analytic; for this

---

[42] Ibid., 200-1.

[43] Ibid., 201.

reason, the scientist can never claim that his own terms have a prophetic function"[44]—not prophetic but for Rieff an act of power, not of truth-seeking.

Skeptical critiques of human knowing often exhibit the same confusions found in Rieff's argument. They react against a simplistic realism. They consider classical theorists of order believers in an ideal, so-called "Platonic" world which contains metaphysical realities such as Eternal Ideas, Forms, or Archetypes. The critical philosopher soon discredits these supposed realities by reminding us that whatever lies outside our own minds remains essentially unknowable. In Nietzsche, appeals to transcendent order suffer further violence when exposed as mere projections of the unconscious psyche. Our resentment, our fear, our eagerness to escape the world that does in fact exist drive us to fabricate another world, the "true" reality, which is not subject to change and suffering. In this we find consolation. But once we become aware of our own complicity in these fabrications, and once we see the reflection of our weakest, most pathetic selves projected onto the screen of the Eternal, our illusions no longer comfort us.

Not only to evaluate Rieff but also to understand Jung, we must come to terms with this problem. All radical critiques of human knowing contain at least a paradox—and I think a contradiction—since our *capacity* to know is supposedly uncovering our *inability* to know. In the context of depth psychology, the question comes to this: Does the discovery of unconscious factors operating in a subject's consciousness controvert the ability to discover those same unconscious factors? A "yes" to this question would end the discussion before it had even started. If the discussion has in fact started and will continue, the answer must be "no." Here we have reached the borderlands of intelligent conversation. If the discovery of the unconscious is in fact a discovery, then intelligent conversation about it is possible and can continue.

An Alternative Hermeneutic

Far from undermining all responsible inquiry, the discovery of the unconscious introduces a more rigorous responsibility towards self-knowledge for those exploring any field. Whether in psychology, philosophy, theology, the natural sciences, or other fields, the investigator who attends to the unconscious factors at work in his or her own psyche is better guarded against introducing bias. Since there is no Archimedean point from which to begin,

[44] Ibid., 234.

no investigator will completely eliminate all bias; but in itself this incompleteness does not negate the possibility of an orientation to truth. False preconceptions may even give rise to a perplexity which induces us to desire understanding. With this possibility in mind, the modern skeptic's disillusionment with the truth-question seems less related to the demise of classical metaphysics than to the demise of Enlightenment epistemology, and less to losing faith in God and "sacred order" than to losing faith in the inflated subject of modernity who fantasizes a discovery of absolutely certain beliefs on which to build philosophical systems.

Recognizing the self-contradiction in Rieff's implicit radical skepticism involves a salutary form of disillusionment, which puts problematic philosophical assumptions to the test. I will now turn to a more recent source for help in understanding fundamental mistakes such as these. In his paper "Language as Horizon?" Frederick Lawrence examines contemporary philosopher Richard Rorty's "sceptical derailment of hermeneutics" in the context of the Boston College conferences at which Hans-Georg Gadamer and Eric Voegelin spoke as featured guests. He shows that in fact Gadamer's position opposes Rorty's, whose errors Lawrence then identifies.[45] This group of errors holds much in common with the underlying theoretical mistakes besetting Rieff's argument. Through understanding the trouble with the epistemologies that have sprung from modernity and through appropriating the alternative hermeneutic presented by Lawrence, we will gain the philosophical grounding with which to evaluate not only Jung's critics, but Jung's psychology itself—its psychological and philosophical context, its theory of symbolic experience, and the possibilities of appropriating this theory for theological use.

Rorty claims to have support from hermeneutics in his influential book, *Philosophy and the Mirror of Nature*, where he proclaims the failure of the modern epistemological project. The quest for certainty regarding human knowledge—clear and distinct foundations which demonstrably reflect an accurate representation of the world—has finally ended with the realization that we have no knowledge of the world which has not been radically conditioned by language. From this realization Rorty concludes that we have no basis for recognizing when we know the truth. We cannot know when our minds have reflected reality accurately. Now that radical skepticism has

[45] Frederick Lawrence, "Language as Horizon," in *The Beginning and the Beyond: Papers from the Gadamer and Voegelin Conferences*, Supplementary Issue of *Lonergan Workshop*, v. 4, ed. Frederick Lawrence (Chico: Scholar's Press, 1984), 13-34.

emerged as the only acceptable model, Rorty envisions a "post-philosophic" culture in which no intelligent person fancies him- or herself able to apply a criterion for truth. With foundationalist epistemology behind us, Rorty imagines that we may now usefully turn our efforts to disciplinary and common sense conversations. Thus we will have migrated "from epistemology to hermeneutics."[46]

Lawrence believes that Rorty has "gravely distorted the point of hermeneutic philosophy." To realize with Gadamer that we only experience the world as mediated by meaning *does* impel us to abandon a naïve view of truth, but this abandoning in no sense warrants the conclusion that the distinctions between various linguistic communities are utterly arbitrary and closed off to rational investigation.

> Yes, the metaphor of "holding up the mirror of nature" may be misleading; the equation of knowledge with either unadulterated sense perception or some explicitly putative intuition of concepts or a reduction to some explicitly formulated first propositions may be as wrong as can be; but that does not warrant Rorty's blatantly Nietzschean assertion that there is "no criterion that we have not created in the course of creating a practice, no standard of rationality that is not an appeal to such a criterion, no rigorous argumentation that is not obedience of our own conventions."[47]

As Roger Brooke has noted, analytical psychology and psychoanalysis have often tended towards a reification of particular psychic phenomena—from complexes to introjected objects. They have not always given due recognition to the limitations of these analogies.[48] Having understood the faults of a literalizing realism, however, we face the important question of whether our conversations, including those which take place in depth psychology, are governed solely by arbitrary conventions. Lawrence thinks not and shows how Gadamer's hermeneutic *therapeia* for modernity reintroduces the truth-question into a post-epistemological world of discourse.

This *therapeia* begins with a diagnosis of what went wrong in modern epistemology: "Epistemology since Descartes and Locke has fallen prey to a set of oversights regarding what actually takes place when we think we are knowing."[49] The false assumptions of these cognitional theories result in a

[46] Ibid., 14-16.

[47] Ibid., 16.

[48] Roger Brooke, "Analytical Psychology and Existential Phenomenology: An Integration and a Clinical Study," *The Psychoanalytic Review* 83:4 (1996): 533.

[49] Lawrence, 17.

misunderstanding that formulates the question about knowing along these lines: "How can subjectivity dwelling within itself (*res cogitans*, and the like) be sure it gets out to, and brings back in, what is really existing out there (*res extensa*, and the like)?"[50] Lawrence describes this formulation as "picture thinking" and outlines its implications: first, we imagine the subject-object split to be ultimately and primordially real; second, we imagine the knowing subject as one who (a) exercises an instrumental use of ideas apart from being situated in a particular context; (b) engages in reflection primarily for "technical" and "calculative" purposes; (c) faces the apparently insoluble problem of whether the "in here" notions created by the mind correspond to a reality "out there"; and (d) is able to know itself only in the manner that it knows other objects.

We easily see the similarity between these implications and the problems found to underlie *The Triumph of the Therapeutic*. Though Rieff distinguishes two types of theory—that of order and that of power—I have shown that he does not in fact treat order in terms of intelligibility and that for him a theory of power is our only legitimate option. It follows quite naturally that he portrays intelligence in instrumental, manipulative terms, including the application of intelligence in psychoanalysis. For instance, he does not contemplate the possibility of an experience of understanding in an analytic setting that we cannot reduce to the dynamics of power and sex but must recognize as an opening of heart and mind. For Rieff, we know ourselves as objects to manipulate. Enlightenment epistemology carries the legacy of its skeptical deformation into his work. He takes for granted the "in here, out there" metaphor for knowing as an accurate description of what takes place in knowing, and the psychological notion that we project inner states onto the other only increases the appeal of radical skepticism. All that we have left to do is to thematize our projections, which may or may not have anything to do with the truth "out there." We will never know. To illuminate the nature of these problems further, I must move on to the alternative which Lawrence proposes.

In contrast to the isolation of the Enlightenment subject from his or her world, for Gadamer the knowing subject begins in the middle of a particular context. There he or she takes up the concrete questions that one must ask in order to choose how to live. The knower then moves on from these practical questions to reflection on both good and bad exemplars and thematizations of what in fact constitutes a good life. As Lawrence explains,

---

[50] Ibid., 18.

> The practical or political question has to do with judging the way one makes sense of one's life. This is the mother-lode or matrix of hermeneutic philosophy's recovery of the truth-question both from epistemology and from technical and scientistic dominance. *Wahrheit und Methode* shows how creating or appreciating a work of art, writing history or carrying out any scholarly investigation are not separated from the finite acts, attitudes, and orientations by which I take up a direction for my life. Indeed, *truth* is at stake in such enterprises. But what is meant by truth here is not primarily faithful description or correct understanding—although Gadamer does not mean to denigrate, disregard, or shirk these dimensions. It is rather truth in relation to Aristotle's *ta heneka*: that for the sake of which everything else is chosen; or, as we would be more likely to express it, what gives meaning to my life. Taking up a way of life means accepting it as true or truly good. Judging the truth of one's life or existence differs from judging the truth of statements because the former sort of judgment actually involves a complex set of operations summarily expressed by Aristotle's practical syllogism: apprehending an end, consenting to it, deliberating concerning means, and choice of the means. A direction in life or a way of life is true, to the degree that it contributes to one's excellence or, as we would say today, one's genuine development and authentic selfhood.[51]

Simply to ask in earnest about the ends for the sake of which one lives already situates the subject in a context not governed solely by convention, but also by the questioning of convention. Yes, each historical and cultural context patterns life in such a way that it will be possible to pursue some human potentialities and nearly impossible to pursue others. But the activity of questioning opens up further horizons for the subject, horizons which may introduce other worthwhile ends that previously were not apparent.

Whereas in Rorty conversation stands in contrast to asking questions, Gadamer includes the movement of questioning in the most authentic forms of human conversation. Yet the first two types of Gadamerian "Thou-experience" mentioned in Lawrence's essay do not exhibit this dynamism. In both, one makes calculative use of knowledge to manipulate the other for one's own purposes. This so-called knowledge, however, is not acquired through an authentic conversation in which one listens attentively to what the other says. It consists in generalities and preconceptions regarding the nature of the other—useful information for egocentric ends. A third type of Thou-experience begins more radically in a state of conscious unknowing. In a sense, one empties the mind of prior claims to knowledge by practicing a fundamental openness that creates a space in which the other may truly be heard: "We only allow others to be themselves in the act of letting them have

[51] Ibid., 19-20.

something to say—not simply in letting them have a voice, but also in granting them a hearing."[52]

Paradoxically, this third type of Thou-experience makes the personal come into being through a kind of impersonality. The openness required is so deep that even apart from the other's personal presence, and apart from his or her persuasiveness, one still has to acknowledge the possible claim against oneself of what in fact has been said. To put it another way, the responsibility to open oneself to what the other has said does not stem from the other. It stems from the subject matter of the conversation. In this manner, an impersonal component of the conversation makes possible the personal nature of the Thou-experience, for without this devotion to the subject at hand, the interpersonal relationship might never amount to anything more than a relationship based on power, utilitarian ends, psychological projections, and the like. Giving someone a hearing is more than simply listening to the words which he or she speaks and understanding what has been signified. It involves an inward turning of attention and an openness of the heart towards matters which may even bring one's own being into question. In other words, an authentic conversation includes the possibility of a challenge to the life that one has in fact chosen as both true and good.

The impersonal or transpersonal element is also present in what for Gadamer is the prime exemplar of conversation—Socratic dialogue with its movement of turning towards assumptions and following them to their rightful conclusions. This form of dialectic always includes the possibility of challenge to the operative assumptions and myths of any culture or of any individual. No wonder Lawrence finds Rorty suspicious of questions, since for Rorty the human being is apparently subjugated by reigning conventions, unable to challenge the current paradigms in a fundamental way. Lawrence shows that emptying conversations of the truth-question endangers the political importance of philosophy. Dialectic in the Socratic-Platonic sense is political because it questions the authority of the common outlooks at work in every person even when those outlooks have a regulatory function in society.

> The overarching convictions or "sense of reality"—one might with justice even say, the catchwords by which we live—often or usually answer the concerns that are other and often more powerful than the concern for *true* meaning and value; and yet at the same time they are subterraneously linked with that concern. Indeed, the dialectic of Socrates appeals to that latent link, and uses it to correct and purify that comprehensive view. So Socratic-Platonic dialectic is the path from the primary, undifferentiated and ambiguous outlook to an adequate view of reality. The heart of

[52] Ibid., 22.

the process of dialectic is both the heart of the attainment of knowledge in general as well as the driving power behind any genuine conversation of dialogue: asking questions.[53]

Unlike Descartes, Socrates does not attempt to withdraw all assent from the beliefs which are part of his context, hoping to find absolutely certain starting points for going on to rebuild a view of the world. This quasi-mathematical model does not accurately convey how the questioning of common assumptions in fact takes place. The conventional sense or senses of reality typically continue to operate in the questioning subject. The movement from an undifferentiated to a more adequate view of reality does not erase tradition's influence, though developments of the personality may prove necessary if we are to live without being held hostage to the authority of conventions.

Dialectic is not a skill in the way that carpentry is a skill. We do not learn a set of standard dialectical techniques that we can apply over and over again in a variety of circumstances to produce clear and predictable solutions. As Lawrence writes, "Questions, in order to be posed, first have to occur to one."[54] We do not know many of the relevant questions for a conversation ahead of time, much less what if any answers will arise. The manner in which questions "occur to one" has a transpersonal character. We do not intentionally come up with the next step in a conversation, as though we knew all along in what direction we intended the conversation to move. That procedure would make for a mere debate, a contest of willpower and persuasive skills. Rather, relevant (and irrelevant) questions arise in consciousness with the apparent cooperation of non-intentional levels of mental organization. The dialectical conversation itself is the condition of knowing, and we exercise an attitude of openness as the virtue that prevents the conversation partners from merely pursuing egocentric ends. Because of this openness to questions, the subject matter itself performs a "tutelage" of the conversation partners. Its transpersonal reality reveals its presence when partners are engaged in pursuit of a truth that "is neither 'mine' nor 'thine.'"

According to Gadamer, fulfillment of the personal and interpersonal goals of the conversation hangs upon the realization of the transpersonal (and, hence, more consistently inter-personal) aims of gaining a common perspective and working out a common language as the elaboration of a common world of meaning. This pursuit,

[53] Ibid.

[54] Ibid.

> this search, is what saves the partners from manipulativeness as well as from extremes of trivialization and fanaticism.[55]

Neither partner knows the outcome of true conversations; it is indeterminate.

For Lawrence and Gadamer, a genuine intention towards truth is "spontaneously operative" in human life. Plato and Aristotle considered this intention the highest of human ends: "It is what pushes the knowing and willing subject beyond itself: it is an immanent principle of self-transcendence."[56] Many factors make cultivating the truth-intention difficult, but these do not discount its reality or the possibility that it can orient a conversation.

> Precisely because of questioning as originative horizon of word, word (or language-in-use) as consciously proceeding an answer may not be compared with a product in the ordinary sense or with anything at one's disposal like instruments or goods for consumption. Far from being the lord and master imposing his dominion over one's world, the questioning person is, in Gadamer's words, "bound to language which is not only the language of the one speaking, but also of the conversation which things hold with us."[57]

We cannot then picture the truth's correspondence to the real as the correspondence of signifiers to some purified set of sense data, nor can we view language-in-use as the purely arbitrary construction of a linguistic community. No simplistic, picture-thinking version of how knowing occurs adequately expresses the complex set of cognitive operations which knowing involves. Questioning is at the heart of these operations, always pushing us beyond "every finite and determined totality" towards a correspondence of knowing with being.[58]

Without the openness that is the "constituent moment of genuine conversation," the horizons of one's world would remain narrow and not allow a further experience of reality to take place. Because of the constituent moment, one's world expands beyond the immediacy of everyday, conventional life and thinking and moves into the wider universe of being. Dialectic takes the role of "midwife to this self-transcending, transpersonal impulse at the core of the truth intention."[59]

---

[55] Ibid., 23-4.

[56] Ibid., 24.

[57] Ibid., 30.

[58] Ibid., 31.

[59] Ibid., 25-6.

> According to Gadamer, questioning at once *supervenes* on experience and *lets* experience *become realized*. It supervenes on experience inasmuch as it arises out of and expresses immediacy in two distinct senses of immediacy: first, in the sense that questioning is provoked by and is about what is immediate *in intentione recta*: the data of sense and/or the (already mediated) immediacy of images, symbols, words, frameworks; secondly, in the sense that questioning itself is a unique expression of a *primordial wonder* (in whatever stage of historical differentiation it may have attained) that is immediate *in intentione obliqua*. Hence, questioning mediates immediacy in both senses; and so it is the mediation *par excellence*.[60]

Two poles are present to consciousness in questioning: the data of sense and of spontaneously generated images, symbols, words, and frameworks to which we explicitly direct our attention; and the primordial wonder which the asking of questions makes present to our self-reflective attention. Knowing itself does not happen spontaneously and become immediately apparent to consciousness. It requires the mediating work of genuine conversations.

Applying this Hermeneutic to Depth Psychology

On the basis of Lawrence's findings, I can now begin the task of challenging the belief that depth psychology is, and can only be, the step-child of radical skepticism in the style of Nietzsche. Radical skepticism is *itself* the step-child of Enlightenment epistemologies. The complexity of language-in-use does not prove that knowing is an irrational, arbitrary business. If we follow Lawrence and Gadamer, we see that despite the complexities of language and context we can still converse in ways that orient us towards truth. We discover that we continue wanting to know the answers to questions about truth, goodness, and "that for the sake of which" we choose a particular way to live. We cannot avoid such questions. Because psychology and psychotherapy also ask such questions—particularly ones focused on how we should live authentically—no matter what we find in Chapter 2 regarding Jung's philosophical assumptions, we must follow Lawrence's guidance. Given the absence of contrary proof, we must assume that questions of truth and goodness belong in psychological conversations about symbolic experience.

In self-awareness and in conversation with others regarding the lives that we each choose, we find a wish to transcend the concrete situations in which pursuit of the human good suffers because of our more abysmal traits. The

---

60 Ibid., 26.

likes of Freud and Nietzsche have made us painfully aware of these traits—the drive to lord it over others, our hidden incestuous desires, the resentment that masquerades as moral superiority, etc. More importantly, they have made us painfully fearful that these dismal potentials are the final truth about human beings and that everything which we considered good in ourselves will be revealed through psychological analysis as repulsive.[61] In Rieff's thought, the only remedy for the abysmal is to enforce moral "control" and occasionally allow for "remission." He wonders what will enforce such controls, since many people no longer submit to the religious authorities. His notion of transcendence would fit quite well in Rorty's post-philosophic culture, where it is impossible to have an uncoerced conversation that orients itself according to the true and the good. This impossibility leaves authoritative control as the only category capable of orienting human life away from the abysmal and destructive. Yet even Rieff's nostalgia for religious authority betrays the persistence in his thought of a quest for the human good beyond mere instinct.

If self-transcending conversations about human ends do occur, then we shall consider them real and need not explain them reductively according to the various motivations presumed to be at work in each conversation partner. Such conversations are as real as any other human activity, no matter how rare their occurrence and no matter what obstacles stand in their way. Control and authority will always be part of an ordered society—this is not at issue. The issue is whether coercion adequately explains experiences of transcendence. In the case of conversation, it does not. The transcending activity of human questioning does not assure by force particular conclusions about religion or morality. It may even threaten authoritative conventions, depending on the divergence of what one discovers from received tradition. Conversation acts as an antidote to merely manipulative applications of intelligence. It opens the mind to a much wider horizon than the one allowed by received conventions. The narrower horizons that we accept on authority can be quite useful, but we should not confuse them with transcendence, because they are subject to dissolution in an open horizon of questioning.

---

[61] There is in fact no reason to draw this conclusion. As Bernard Lonergan comments in *Insight*, the morally repugnant features which arise in dreams are not the final truth about our natures. They are latent potentialities which both waking and dream life typically reject. Bernard Lonergan, *Insight: A Study of Human Understanding*, 5th ed., ed. Frederick E. Crowe and Robert M. Doran, v. 3 in the *Collected Works of Bernard Lonergan* (Toronto: University of Toronto Press, 1992), 230.

In fact, Jung considered the lagging of moral development far behind technological development a central problem of modernity. Contrary to Rieff's characterization of Jung as an antinomian Romanticist, he wanted to know how moral and psychological development might continue after the demise of Christendom's hegemony: "As [modern man's] consciousness has broadened and differentiated, so his moral nature has lagged behind."[62] Correctly or not, he believed that psychology actually aided the development of moral awareness.

We will find that Rieff has wrongly claimed that the only possible goal left in Jung is personal well-being. On the contrary, Jung considers the ego's well-being as only one possible *telos* among many. His keen sense of non-ego factors in the psyche—factors that may jeopardize the feeling of well-being—make him well aware of the powerful claims they make.[63] In Jung's psychology, human beings contain a plurality of psychic levels of organization; and consciousness faces the task of wrestling with these powers and through this exchange of finding a workable adaptation to the everyday environment of life.[64] For Jung, a strong ego enables one to bring moral concerns at the personal and interpersonal levels to bear on the transpersonal aspects of symbolic experience, which he considers morally ambivalent.[65] He certainly did not believe that the self should be freed from all restraints. There is no naïve Romanticism in Jung—a strong Romantic influence, yes, but not of the sort that Rieff suggests. We must remember the level-headed, practical Jung, as well as the Romantic Jung. This level-headed Jung had spent too many years treating chronic schizophrenics to nurse illusions that the unconscious is a beneficent deity.

---

[62] C.G Jung, "The Undiscovered Self," in *Civilization in Transition*, v. 10, 2nd ed., trans. R.F.C. Hull, in *The Collected Works of* C.G. *Jung*, ed. Herbert Reed, Michael Fordham, and Gerhard Adler, exec. ed. William McGuire, Bollingen Series XX (Princeton: Princeton University Press, 1970), § 574.

[63] C.G Jung, "Transformation Symbolism in the Mass," in *Psychology and Religion: West and East*, v. 11, 2nd ed., trans. R.F.C. Hull, in *The Collected Works of* C.G. *Jung*, ed. Herbert Reed, Michael Fordham, and Gerhard Adler, exec. ed. William McGuire, Bollingen Series XX (Princeton: Princeton University Press, 1968), § 391.

[64] C.G. Jung, "The Relations between the Ego and the Unconscious," in *Two Essays on Analytical Psychology*, v. 7, 2nd ed., trans. R.F.C. Hull, in *The Collected Works of* C.G. *Jung*, ed. Herbert Reed, Michael Fordham, and Gerhard Adler, exec. ed. William McGuire, Bollingen Series XX (Princeton: Princeton University Press, 1966), § 240.

[65] C.G. Jung, "A Psychological View of Conscience," CW *10*, § 845.

We can discern the assumption behind Rieff's accusation that Jung is morally remissive; it is that true religious commitment can happen only within the context of obedience to authority. Many religious people would strongly object to this mischaracterization. Rieff and the hermeneuts of suspicion neglect the fact that the activity of questioning itself—including putting questions to sources of religious authority—is a constitutive moment in an experience of transcendence. The self-transcending philosophical quest asks questions in a way that differentiates but does not cut off questions of understanding and judgment from the affective experience of symbols. Of course, depth psychology does by its nature contain an element of "suspicion" towards religious beliefs. It analyzes how human beings project aspects of themselves onto the other, including the divine Other. Jung knows about this quandary. He had nothing to say about the God beyond projections, he asserts, but much to say about the many god-images which appear on the level of psychic phenomena.[66] Chapter 2 will provide the occasion to discuss the philosophical background to these problems more thoroughly.

In Rieff's view, Jung advised elaborating symbolic experience through "fantasy" as part of his illusionist repertoire, which offers escapism as consolation for a world empty of divine presences. In Chapter 3, I will show that fantasy in Jung does not offer escape; it offers an opportunity to develop greater awareness of the emotionally difficult dynamics of the unconscious. Lawrence defined "symbols" as part of the "already-mediated immediacy" of consciousness. I understand him to mean that while symbolic images themselves occur with near spontaneity and directness to conscious awareness, their meaning is not similarly immediate but requires our conscious participation to flesh out symbolic meanings. In psychology, one fleshes out this meaning through asking questions, attempting interpretations, paying attention to affect, interacting in an analytic relationship where the symbol is discussed, and engaging in some kind of imaginative play or fantasy—the painting of dream images, imaginal dialogues with inner figures, etc.—which Jungians refer to as active imagination.[67] Through these activities we come to know the meanings of a symbol. Since we can only accomplish such work when open to a high intensity of difficult emotion, we have no reason on the face of things to call it escapism.

Playful mediation of psychic contents to awareness does go against the grain of our reigning Western sense of reality, our "scientific common sense,"

---

[66] C.G. Jung, "Foreword to White's 'God and the Unconscious,'" *CW 11*, § 454.

[67] See the definition of fantasy in *CW 6*, § 713.

which is still very much infused with mechanistic, deterministic, and materialistic assumptions that some scientists have in fact shed. But we cannot label those who dare to look beyond this limited sense of reality escapists. Like Nietzsche revolting against the "world-denying" religionist, Rieff revolts against the value Jung gives to the inner life and its realities, which have no clear use for the modern, world-conquering, heroic ego. Such realities call into question the world-transforming modernists' exclusive claim to a worthwhile set of values. They bring us into relation—in part, through symbolic experience—with the affects and attachments that ground our sense of what we consider good and valuable.

Concluding Remarks

By the end of the book, I will be arguing that like the Socratic quest (Gadamer, Lawrence), the symbolic quest (Jung) takes place in human beings for whom an intention towards truth has become a formative reality in their lives. Both quests introduce the self-transcending principle of the truth-intention to the work of life. For Jung's psychology of symbol formation, we will find that the implications of living symbolically extend far beyond the narcissistic pursuit of personal well-being over all else. Other satisfactions often pull us more deeply not through external coercion but through spontaneously arising desires for many non-ego ends for whose sake we live. Symbolic work engenders an openness to these desires, which often arise concomitantly with symbols mediating affective states from the depth of the psyche.

The eclipse of the authority that traditional religious institutions once had *does* change the religious landscape. Yet despite whatever social and moral disorientation the eclipse has caused, we have no *a priori* reason to side with Rieff and understand religion as at heart a matter of authority and control. The psychological study of symbol formation will help us begin to provide grounds for understanding a religiously ordered life as other than unquestioned reliance on external authority.

Rieff thinks that the application of reason to religion generates a shift from illusion to the hard facts of science. Depth psychology methodically applies reason to the human subject's relation through symbols to levels of psychic organization that exist apart from what is readily accessible to consciousness. Unless we find otherwise, we need not consider this turn of attention deadly to religious commitment. We will move forward with a different model, one that understands the psychological turn of attention as one aspect of a development from compact, mythological consciousness to differentiated consciousness. That is, we will understand it as a development through which consciousness discovers its ability not only to participate in the flow of symbol formation but also to maintain its distinction from the flow and simultaneously reflect on the symbols rather than being reduced to a passive recipient.

I have identified some of the questions relevant for a theological appropriation of analytical psychology's understanding of symbolic experience. Rieff does make an important concession about Jung, namely, that Jung saw the inevitability of the religious function better than Freud did.[68] If this religious function remains an inevitable part of human life, then presumably the modern attempts to stamp it out will fail. The decline of religious authorities then do not announce an end to religion, but a shift away from a strictly hierarchical model. A post-religious culture is ultimately no more possible than a post-philosophic culture, for both religious and philosophical quests begin spontaneously in human experience; and when they are repressed, they will presumably arise again in some other form. In the next chapter, I will investigate the historical influences on Jung's work—both from psychology and philosophy.

---

[68] *Triumph*, 90.

▪ C H A P T E R T H R E E ▪

The Historical Sources of Jung's Psychology

The preceding chapter raised some of the basic philosophical issues pertinent to the rise of depth psychology. I will now distinguish between two questions: (a) what was Jung's own philosophical position? and (b) what philosophical position(s) will today support and explain his discoveries? Chapter 1 made preliminary suggestions with regard to (b) by proposing a hermeneutic that takes the spontaneous intention to truth into account. I will develop this line of thinking further in later chapters. In the present chapter, I will concentrate on (a)—a question concerning the history of philosophy and psychology—and proceed by investigating the following aspects of this background material: first, Jung's philosophical lineage of neo-Kantian subjectivism; second, the influence of biological vitalism; third, the teleological nature of his prospective method; fourth, the impossibility of avoiding the metaphysical questions that arise in depth psychology; fifth, the importance of emphasizing Jung's place in the hermeneutical tradition of human rather than natural science; and, finally, the basis for Jung's thought in the clinical and experimental traditions of dynamic psychiatry.

Jung was not a trained philosopher. He was a psychiatrist who had been reading philosophy since early in his adult life, and he makes frequent references in his writings to philosophers—particularly to Kant, Nietzsche, and Schopenhauer. Unfortunately for us, nowhere does he give a clear, extended treatment of basic philosophical questions. He simply makes statements throughout the *Collected Works* that are characteristic of his views. We have no reason to assume from the outset that taken together these statements create a well-defined and consistent standpoint. Jung was suspicious of systematic precision. He thought that such precision falsified reality by trying to find simple definitions for what is in fact elusively complex. We must therefore identify a variety of standpoints and influences and then consider them as a whole.

To approach this difficult historical question, I will begin with Marilyn Nagy's book, *Philosophical Issues in the Psychology of C.G. Jung.*[69] Many authors with roots in analytical psychology follow in the intuitive, meandering style of Jung himself, but Nagy attempts to bring clarity through a historical inquiry: "Though Jung never delineated a formal epistemological position it is possible, by following a developmental time line, and by studying a large number of his statements about what we know, to obtain a consistent picture of his views." She concludes that

> the conceptual structure of Jung's psychology is based on philosophical postulates which express an idealist and a metaphysical view of reality. Analytical psychology is a position-taking on philosophical issues of the nineteenth century.... Because he found a *psychological* format for idealism which could lead into the twentieth century, Jung himself became the latest in a tradition of great idealist philosophers to have a powerful influence in the culture of their times.[70]

Nagy situates Jung in the controversies between scientific and religious world views that took place in the 19th and early 20th centuries. She believes that he came down squarely on the side of those—particularly the metaphysical idealists—who considered the new scientific views of life to be unacceptably reductive, mechanistic, and threatening to both religion and morality. His two main sources were idealist philosophy itself and vitalistic biological theories. The vitalists argued against a reduction of life to chance or mechanism, and Jung "maintained vitalist convictions throughout his life, in flat opposition to the view of organic process which forms the basis of biological studies."[71]

The Young Metaphysician

While at the University of Basel, Jung joined a club whose members held lectures and disputations. His own talks to this society are published as the "Zofingia Lectures" in a supplementary volume to the *Collected Works.*[72] Here

[69] Marilyn Nagy, *Philosophical Issues in the Psychology of C.G. Jung* (Albany: State University of New York Press, 1991).

[70] Ibid., 265.

[71] Ibid., 266-7.

[72] C.G Jung, *The Zofingia Lectures*, supplementary volume A, ed. William McGuire, trans. Jan van Heurck, in *The Collected Works of C.G. Jung*, ed. Herbert Reed, Michael

we see a young medical student in the grip of questions about the soul. Nagy uses these early talks to bolster her argument that Jung's thought makes metaphysical claims even at its earliest stages, despite his frequent protestations to the contrary. She also identifies the early contours of Jung's lifelong philosophical position. It shows itself in the lectures, re-emerges in writings after the break with Freud, and charts a course of development for his psychology: "Jung's earliest convictions were also his last ones."[73]

The Zofingia lectures went unpublished for many years. Most readers did not know of them until the historian of psychology Henri Ellenberger discovered that the manuscripts still existed. When they were finally published in English in 1983, scholars of Jung could no longer begin with the experimental studies that he conducted while at the famous Burghölzli psychiatric hospital, and certainly not with work done during his friendship with Freud. The lectures themselves date from 1896-1899. They offer substantial evidence of his earliest ideas beyond the autobiographical contemplations of *Memories, Dreams, Reflections*.

The striking exuberance of the lectures never allows the reader to forget the centrality of religious questions in Jung's life. He attacks rationalism in theology and reductive materialism in science. In the first and second lectures, "The Border Zones of Exact Science" (1896) and "Some Thoughts on Psychology" (1897), he deals primarily with mechanistic science by arguing that it fails to explain the emergence of life and consciousness. The hard-line reductionists in German physiology, the "Berlin Group," had attempted to free biology from metaphysical assumptions by rooting out the influence of vitalism. Their public success reflected itself in a well-known speech given by Emil Du Bois-Reymond in 1872 to an assembly in Leipzig of the German Naturalists and Physicians. There he outlined the limits of human knowledge with the statement that while we will never know what matter or mind are in themselves, we must assume the fact of a perceiving mind which is able to know matter in motion.[74]

In opposition, Jung rails against the scientific authorities who close off immaterial realities from investigation. Psychology, he argues, must not limit itself to the study of matter in motion. It should study the human soul and

Fordham, and Gerhard Adler, exec. ed. William McGuire, Bollingen Series XX (Princeton: Princeton University Press, 1983).

[73] Nagy, 12.

[74] Ibid., 13.

come to know that it exists independently of space and time.[75] He relies on evidence from the popular but controversial areas of spiritualism, hypnotism, and parapsychology. If we encounter mysterious phenomena, we should put aside the dogmas of physiological reductionism and conduct a scientific investigation. Nagy points out the importance for Jung of Kant's essay, *Dreams of a Spirit Seer*, in which he reflects on Emmanuel Swedenborg's reported "remote vision" of a terrible fire in Stockholm. Jung apparently did not absorb Kant's reservations about the story, but came away with a bolstered sense that we need not exclude evidence of immaterial realities from scientific work.

In these lectures he also opposes the radical subjectivist interpreters of Kant. They believed that the imputation of teleology to nature is a projection of human values onto the world. Jung considers this a counsel of despair. He argues that the moral consciousness which Kant outlines in his ethical writings creates a sound basis for knowing something real. According to Nagy, Jung is not simply recommending a therapeutic lie as an antidote to purposelessness and despair. He believes that our wills are free and that innate moral knowledge brings us "as close as is humanly possible to knowledge of reality in itself."[76]

Tempering Metaphysical Inclinations with a Pragmatic Standpoint

As evidenced in the first version (1912) of the book later revised to become *Symbols of Transformation* (1952), Jung changed his early views and adopted a split between the inner world of moral value and the outer world of fact. Here a pragmatic concern for psychological health quite clearly motivates his preference for inner reality. In short, religious beliefs perform a protective function, and human flourishing surely benefits from belief in a provident God and in the intrinsic value of life. Faith protects us from debilitating nihilism. But if we accept religious beliefs as true, we are remaining in a state of infantile dependence. Jung's solution is to appreciate the beauty and meaning of religious symbols without investing naïve faith in them.[77]

By 1912 he was under the influence of Freud, whose rigorous skepticism towards faith no doubt brought Jung's religious views closer to a religion

---

[75] *Zofingia*, 31-2, 38.

[76] Nagy, 15-19.

[77] Ibid., 24-5.

within the limits of reason alone. His dissertation work on the psychology of occult phenomena also engendered a more questioning attitude. This study focuses on a cousin of his who conducted séances. She was the medium. Jung participated in these séances, and the relationship between the two was intense. It eventually became clear that the spirits were revealing a romantic attachment to Jung.[78]

According to F.X. Charet, Jung attempted to reconcile his fascination with spiritualistic phenomena to his scientific and rational commitments. He made this attempt first through the philosophical discourses of the Zofingia lectures, in which he argues that the soul transcends space and time. Secondly, he turned in his dissertation to the psychiatric study of mediums. Theodore Flournoy had pioneered such studies. Jung takes the position that psychology allows us to identify multiple centers of personality in some mediums. It further shows that the mediumistic expression of these fragments is an attempt by the psyche to heal itself from its fragmentation.[79] Even when understood psychologically, spiritualism therefore goes beyond mere superstition. A true psychic reality—a spiritual or incorporeal reality—is at work, though not the world of departed souls which spiritualists believe in.

The Resurgence of Metaphysics in Jung's Psychology

In Jung's writings from his "Freudian" period, psychological or "psychic" reality refers to meaningful inner experience over against the world of matter in motion. This position is not far from the one that Rieff imputes to Jung. In Nagy's view, Jung then changed his philosophical attitude a second time, soon after the break with Freud. The separation between the outer world of fact and the inner world of value, the scientifically real and the emotionally real, gave way to the same affirmation of the soul's incorporeal but scientifically evident reality that we see in the Zofingia lectures.

78 John Kerr, *A Most Dangerous Method: The Story of Jung, Freud, and Sabina Speilrein* (New York: Alfred A. Knopf, 1993), 50-1.

79 F.X. Charet, *Spiritualism and the Foundations of C.G. Jung's Psychology* (Albany: State University of New York Press, 1993), 43, 125, 163.

He returned to this affirmation on the basis of his prospective interpretation of dreams and fantasies.[80] In this method, one discovers purposiveness in dreams by asking questions of final rather than efficient cause. To what end does this dream point the dreamer? Does it reveal a development in the personality? Jung is well aware that for those who think efficient causality sufficiently explains dreams, his method seems to recommend regression into fantasy. Yet he insists that only the teleological point of view can do justice to the meaning of some dreams. Developments do occur in a personality, and sometimes dreams prefigure these changes. If we limit ourselves to uncovering the supposedly fundamental prior causes, we will miss the real, ordering effect that a dream and its interpretation can have in the individual's existence.[81]

When Jung emerged from the personal crisis of the years following his break with Freud, his insistence on the reality of the soul had grown stronger. Once again he challenged materialism and determinism, yet this time he relied on a philosophical standpoint very similar to post-Kantian subjectivism. As Nagy states,

> But more and more, his appeal for the inner life was based not on the ethical value of recognizing an alternative to the objective, scientific view, nor on the prophylactic value for the patient, but on an *epistemological assumption* that the *only* certainty we have is our knowledge of the inner world. We are in fact imprisoned in the symbolic realm of the psyche.... Therefore, Jung concludes (though these are not his own words), we might just as well trust our inner feelings and our inner experience since that is all there is to know. If we do not trust it, what religious faith in life we do have will be infantile and dependent on someone else's authority. If we do trust it, we have

---

[80] I will use "dreams," "fantasies," and "unconscious contents" as shorthand to indicate the sequences of image and story that arise during dream sleep and during what Jung describes as "active imagination." In active imagination, one uses drawing, painting, imaginary dialogue, or some other medium to flesh out a dimly apprehended feeling or idea. In this kind of communication with oneself, the "nondirected thinking" that is taking place at the threshold of consciousness is mediated to awareness in symbolic forms. Further, this nondirected thinking constitutes a natural function of the human psyche. See Ann Belford Ulanov and Barry Ulanov, *Religion and the Unconscious* (Philadelphia: The Westminster Press, 1975), 27. My third chapter will focus on this function.

[81] Nagy, 26-7.

a chance that our lives may be governed by the kind of "'legitimate' faith ...[which] must always rest on experience."[82]

In short, knowledge of the material world takes place only through an experience in the soul. The objective knowledge of empirical science therefore cannot claim to describe reality more accurately than the soul's experience of purpose and value describes it. Jungians have used this "subjectivist argument" again and again to defend analytical psychology and its clinical practice. In Nagy's view, it is unnecessary and makes nonsense of the scientific enterprise, for it fundamentally rejects knowledge of physical reality. It also reveals Jung's idealism: "To believe in these dictates of the soul rather than in the physical evidence of the perceivable world has been the purport of every metaphysical idealist since Plato."[83]

Jung's Subjectivist Argument

While Nagy looks very favorably on the practical wisdom offered by Jung's psychology, she believes that his mature philosophical position amounts in effect to a set of religious beliefs, a faith in the reality of the psyche. Jung left Freud and returned to the soul—"to the life of the inner feelings"—but he did not stop at an assertion of the central moral importance of feeling. He went on to relativize the objectivity of science in order to secure his subjective standpoint against challenges. This was Jung's Tertullian-like sacrifice of the intellect, his leap to faith in metaphysical reality. Nagy uses the word "metaphysical" in much the same way that Jung does. For both, it means knowledge about things-in-themselves beyond empirical phenomena and includes knowledge of God, the archetypes, and other transcendent realities. Nagy lists the typical points in Jung's subjectivist argument:[84]

- There are two styles of knowing, extraversion and introversion. Extraverted types are primarily oriented towards external objects. Introverted types are primarily oriented towards internal ideas. Introverts have the epistemological upper hand for Jung, because no one knows an external object apart from internal ideas about that object.

[82] Ibid., 29-30.

[83] Ibid., 31.

[84] Ibid., 33-6.

- All knowledge is uncertain, and psychological knowledge especially so, because its object of study is identical with the subject doing the studying. It has no point of reference outside the psyche.
- It is perfectly legitimate to treat the psyche itself as real, because every field of knowledge depends on the psyche's ability to know things.
- Though all objects of knowledge must be mediated in a psychological form, we can in some sense experience the psyche itself directly. Images, ideas, and other psychic contents make up the immediate reality of the psyche.
- The unknown, unconscious matrix out of which consciousness arises is in fact the true substance of all that exists. This late speculation fulfills the metaphysical trajectory towards idealist monism that Nagy finds in the beginnings of Jung's thought.

In various combinations and reiterations, these five points make up Jung's subjectivist argument. They all show skepticism about knowing things-in-themselves and a preference for inner experience over empirical data.

This preference opens Jung to the charge of countering materialism with another type of reductionism—one which reduces everything, including God, to subjective psychological experiences. This was Martin Buber's objection. In his opinion, Jung had eliminated from religion the I-Thou relationship between a finite person and transcendent being. Michael Palmer argues that Jung takes pains to refute this charge, but is unable to do so effectively using the terms of his own system. The subjective argument shields religion from attacks by the materialists; on the other hand, it leaves the distinction between God and psychological images of God unclear.[85] Jung would probably counter by saying that examining God-images and positing their archetypal source in the objective psyche is the best that psychology can do. It cannot go further into questions of transcendent being. This response has a common sense value, since he was primarily attempting to bring attention to our religious experiences themselves. Nevertheless, to wonder about a something or someone not intrinsically limited by all the conditions of our own finite existence *is itself* a religious experience with psychological implications. It can certainly bring about a sense of the numinous.

Nagy argues that Jung's skepticism about knowing things-in-themselves, whether transcendent or immanent, grew out of a general climate of suspicion about knowledge in the second half of the 19th century. Kant came into

---

[85] Michael Palmer, *Freud and Jung on Religion* (New York: Routledge, 1997), 195.

vogue—particularly his first critique. Each philosophical camp used Kantian epistemology to attack its opponent's claims. Positivists appealed to Kant in their denial of transcendent realities, and idealists in their denial of material things-in-themselves.[86] These appeals were based largely on the neo-Kantianism of thinkers such as Hermann von Helmholtz, Friedrich Albert Lange, and Erich Adickes. In Nagy's words, "If matter exists only within our consciousness, then all objects of the psyche have equal right to be called 'real.' For Jung, as for Adickes, and for the phenomenal idealists in general, a skeptical, subjectivist interpretation of Kant's epistemology serves as a defense against reduction to matter."[87] This point is not only epistemological; it is also historical. Nagy has shown that Jung's subjectivist argument did not arise out of clinical experience. He took on the philosophical position of the idealists and thus chose sides in the great debate between science and religion. To side with the idealists was to choose religion, morality, God, and inner values over against mechanism, determinism, and the absolute authority of the natural sciences.

The Influence of Vitalism

Not every biologist accepted a mechanistic, deterministic understanding of life. Hans Driesch studied biology under Ernst Haeckel and began his scientific career committed to the mechanistic views of his master. Yet his work in the laboratory introduced a fundamental challenge to these views. Driesch discovered that the fertilized egg of a sea urchin, if divided when it reached two or four blastomeres, would develop into two or four individual sea urchins. According to the prevailing, mechanistic views, this development should have been impossible. Each cell in an embryo was thought to play an indispensably unique role in the life of the organism. If one cell were removed, the organism would no longer function. It would disintegrate, just as machines disintegrate when a mechanical part is removed. Instead, each divided blastomere went on to become a complete sea urchin.

Evidently, Driesch reasoned, an organism is quite different from a machine. He also concluded from his experiment that some form of teleology operates in living organisms. Something must move these beings towards wholeness. Since we cannot observe this something directly, he thought that it

---

[86] Nagy, 64.

[87] Ibid., 72.

must be an immaterial reality. He named this reality "entelechy" and described the nature of its presence as "psychoid." Entelechy passed itself down from one generation to the next. Driesch attempted to distance his theory from traditional metaphysics, but Nagy considers it "clear that what Driesch has in mind is a God concept based upon the experience of the individual as an organized and purposing being." According to Nagy, this aspect of vitalism is a key source for the notion of individuation, Jung's own teleological theory of human development. He even uses the term "psychoid" in late works to mean an element which bridges the material and immaterial aspects of human nature.[88]

Jung's theory of individuation draws on the notion of libido. He believes that sexual drives are an important but not exclusive aspect of libido, which he defines more generally as "psychic energy," the energy that moves the organism towards further organization.[89] This energy can either propel human development forward or falter and cause regression to an archaic, primitive level of the psyche. Such regression constitutes a psychosis. Freud and Jung argued about whether displacements of sexual energy can account for both neurotic and psychotic illnesses, but for Nagy this is not where the two diverge most fundamentally. Instead, the difference is philosophical:

> I am certain that what was really at stake between the two men in their struggle over the nature of psychic libido was the ancient mind-body problem as it surfaces in the biological sphere. For the person who believes in a final reduction of life processes to the properties of inorganic matter it is always a problem to explain the unique facts of human consciousness ("the reality function"), human creativity, and human culture. Freud proposed that survival entails compromise and struggle and that culture and consciousness are accidents of the evolutionary process.
>
> For the person who believes in God and in the transcendent qualities of the human mind which intuits God's existence, the problem is to explain how it happens that human beings are connected to lower life forms and to the dead matter of the earth they inhabit. The usual solution to this dilemma has been sought by declaring that life itself is unique—that there is a break-off (or a break-in) point where life forms intervene in the accidental course of activity in the universe, and that life forms themselves may be seen as developing or evolving in an unconscious but purposeful fashion toward ever higher forms of consciousness.
>
> This is the program which has been undertaken by the vitalistic biologists (Driesch and others), by theories of emergent evolution (Morgan and Alexander) and by the

[88] Ibid., 247-9, 250-7.

[89] C.G. Jung, "On the Psychology of the Unconscious," in CW 7, §§ 74-8.

> process philosophers (Whitehead) in a modified form. For them, mind and purpose are present with life itself.[90]

Jung is on the side of the metaphysically inclined. Psychic energy itself has intentionality, and the basic reality that moves human development forward is not material, but immaterial.

Individuation and the Prospective Method

Leaving aside the idealist-materialist debate for a moment, let us turn to Jung's phenomenology of the psyche's prospective function. He believes that dream images prefigure and encourage healthy psychological development, and he finds clues of developmental direction even in the symptoms of a disorder: "the symptom, the fantasy image, and the dream have an objective and directive significance for the individual."[91] The goal of psychological development is individuation, the coming-into-being of a person whose characteristics are somehow contained from the beginning as unconscious potentials.[92] Psychotherapy cures by freeing a stuck process of individuation. Symptoms give indications of the disturbance, and the prospective method uses dreams and their interpretation to resolve the problem.

Jung argues that the tendency towards wholeness has a symbolic counterpart, which he calls the "self."[93] Symbols of the self communicate a sense of the entirety of the psyche's reality, a reality far beyond what individual personal identity can contain. Yet because we experience the self as numinous, its affective power helps resolve disorder, especially in moderns who have lost

---

[90] Nagy, 128.

[91] Ibid., 137-9.

[92] Ibid., 209.

[93] Although "self" is often capitalized in the literature, I will follow the *Collected Works* and use the lower case. In German, "das Selbst" better communicates the impersonality of this notion, while in my mind "self" or "Self" tends to communicate a mistaken meaning of a transcendent, perfected human ego. For Jung, the self symbolically sums up the full reality of the psyche, including transpersonal levels that normally have little part in conscious awareness. See C.G. Jung, *Aion: Researches into the Phenomenology of the Self*, v. 9ii, 2nd ed., trans. R.F.C. Hull, in *The Collected Works of C.G. Jung*, ed. Herbert Reed, Michael Fordham, and Gerhard Adler, exec. ed. William McGuire, Bollingen Series XX (Princeton: Princeton University Press, 1979), §§ 43-67.

a living connection to the numinous.[94] Among other things, self-symbols in Jung relate to the rather mundane fact that we are constantly enacting certain potentialities in our being and leaving aside others.[95] Self-symbols express a larger spectrum of possible developments for us to enact through a directed choice of one direction in life over another. We need reminding that we often do not know what is possible in our development as persons, and symbols and their interpretation act as these reminders.[96]

Peter Homans understands the question of a human *telos* as the crucial point of contention between Jung and Freud:

> Freud rejected the notion outright: the unconscious had (was) an "arche" but not a "telos." It referred back to infanthood but not forward to maturity. On the other hand, Jung sought to wed archeology and teleology: the primary task of therapy was to activate the life-affirming and self-constructing forces buried in the unconscious.... We should also recognize that Freud did not so much reject Jung's view of teleology as he did the idea itself, in whatever form. The explanation for this should by now be obvious: teleology is implicated in culture-making. In short, for Jung psychotherapy was culture-making at the individual level.[97]

Freud strenuously attempted to distinguish psychoanalysis from a value-laden quest for cultural foundations. He wanted to establish its scientific credentials; and according to the reigning paradigm, science had to do with fundamental mechanistic causes. Any appeal to higher sources of organization was an appeal to religion and values. Yet as Homans observes, contemporary psychoanalysis shows a return of Jung's view. In particular, such thinkers as Winnicott, Milner, and Kohut developed theories in which play, illusion, and creativity have a clearly teleological role in personal development. Their followers have begun to realize the full implications of this shift in recent work on narrative and intersubjectivity, even though they avoid references to Jung or to the forbidden term "teleology." I will return to these interesting changes in contemporary psychoanalysis in Chapter 4.

---

[94] Lionel Corbett, *The Religious Function of the Psyche* (New York: Routledge, 1996), 13.

[95] Joseph F. Rychlak, "Jung as Dialectician and Teleologist," in *Jung in Modern Perspective*, ed. Renos K. Papadopoulos and Graham S. Saayman (Hounslow, Middlesex: Wildwood House, 1984), 49.

[96] Murray Stein, *Jung's Treatment of Christianity: The Psychotherapy of a Religious Tradition* (Wilmette, IL: Chiron Publications, 1985), 49.

[97] Peter Homans, *Jung in Context: Modernity and the Making of a Psychology*, Second Edition (Chicago: University of Chicago Press, 1995), xxxvi.

From the Prospective Method to a Metaphysics of Archetypes

We cannot separate Jung's prospective method and theory of individuation from their grounds in the practices of psychotherapy. The method and theory do not simply follow as deductions from his philosophical assumptions. Nevertheless, the practical level naturally leads to philosophical questions. To ask what a dream wants from the dreamer would strike materialistically inclined modern thinkers as peculiar. To venture meaningful interpretations of a dream is one thing; to believe that the dream is venturing interpretations of the individual is quite another thing. It was not long before his use of the prospective method led Jung to wonder about structures in the psyche that would explain the goal-directedness of unconscious material. The practice needed a theory, and Nagy argues that he eventually "hypostatized" primordial images by creating his theory of archetypes. Archetypes are the structural determinants of the unconscious: "Here is Jung's answer to Freud; libido is rooted in archetypes, not in the drive forces of the sexual libido."[98] This is metaphysics, she says, reiterating her overarching thesis that Jung was not the empiricist he claimed to be, but a metaphysician who created a depth psychological version of idealist philosophy.[99]

Nagy is one of the few authors to treat the historical sources for archetypal theory with critical acumen. But she is not the first to relate this theory to Plato's notion of the Forms; and she believes that both thinkers share a judgment that the "ultimate structure of reality lies not in the materially observable strata of the universe, but at a non-material level to which only our minds (or our feelings) are witness...."[100] Both had religious and moral reasons for these beliefs. Simply put, a transcendent point of view encourages those seeking a good and meaningful life. Nagy appears to accept the modern division of fact from value, for she admires the moral feeling of "idealists" such as Plato and Jung but cautiously avoids the judgment that such feelings reflect reality in the sense of observable fact. They are inward realities which

---

[98] Nagy, 143.

[99] Various theories of evolutionary biology were tremendously influential in the late 1800s. Frank Sulloway argues that Freud's claim to base psychoanalytic theory purely on empirical psychological data is false. Freud fails to acknowledge his debt to evolutionary biology. Frank J. Sulloway, *Freud, Biologist of the Mind: Beyond the Psychoanalytic Legend* (New York: Basic Books, 1979), 425.

[100] Nagy, 158.

the individual feels emotionally convinced of and insists on "against the evidences of the senses."[101]

Nagy also points to Jung's reliance on Schopenhauer for support of belief in immaterial realities. He uses Schopenhauer's theory of generative Ideas as a model for the theory of archetypes. Both theories describe immaterial realities that act with real force in the real world. Yet Schopenhauer's Ideas act blindly, and Jung's archetypes act in a developmentally goal-directed way.[102] Jung needed a further warrant for this insistence on teleology, argues Nagy, and he finds this warrant in God. Though we cannot know God or any other thing-in-itself, we must posit their existence, because our subjective experiences have to refer to something if they are to make sense. Though Jung insists that we know nothing of God apart from our images of the divine, he thinks it quite necessary and responsible to believe in God. Nagy explains the four basic arguments that he uses to make his case for theism: (1) the old "common consent" argument which states that theism is ancient and universal; (2) a Kantian attitude whereby for moral reasons we must think and act *as though* God exists; (3) the necessity of intellectual humility and openness to a transcendent reality beyond what we can experience as an object; and (4) a form of the ontological argument that moves from our experiences of the divine to its existence.[103]

In addition to the philosophical and theological sources, Jung based archetypal theory on ideas from biology and related fields. The heritage of vitalism again plays a key role. Ernst Haeckel put forward his (now widely discredited) "biogenetic law," which states that the historical, evolutionary development of a phylum is evident in the development of an individual organism of that class: ontogeny recapitulates phylogeny. In the development of the individual towards maturity, we observe in progressive stages what had been the adult forms of such organisms in the evolutionary past. For instance, the brain development reached by a human fetus at the beginning of week x of pregnancy recapitulates the brain development of an adult human ancestor from y millions of years ago.

Transposed into depth psychology, this law appears to support the theory that archetypes in some sense express human prehistory by bringing it into the

---

[101] Ibid., 161. Nagy's view of Plato reflects the modern tendency to consider the changeable, historical world as reality, and the eternal world as a projected illusion—quite the opposite of the conclusion that Plato in fact reached.

[102] Ibid., 164.

[103] Ibid., 151-3.

present moment of our experience. Jung thus considered archetypes as stored vestiges of prior forms of human consciousness from the evolutionary past. The evidence does not clearly indicate whether Jung fully accepted Haeckel's law, but Nagy believes that the phylogenic standpoint clearly contributed to the birth of archetypal theory.[104]

To Nagy, in sum, Jung's theories regarding the soul's reality and the purposive, archetypal structure of life imply a metaphysics and even a theology: "This is God talk. That, at least, is the term most usually applied in Western philosophical thought to indicate supraordinate, intending mind."[105] In this God talk, Jung pairs the instincts with their spiritual concomitants, the archetypes, in such a way that human values become part of the structure of reality itself. Furthermore, the prospective method activates instinctual-archetypal levels of the psyche for the sake of individuation, that is, personal, moral, and religious maturation. In taking this position, Jung contradicts those who consider adaptive survival to be the only scientifically acceptable notion of purpose in the instinctual behavior of human beings.[106]

Jung and the Paracelsian Theory of Knowledge

Most of what Nagy has discovered about Jung's philosophy derives from elucidating the historical sources behind his works. He rarely makes statements that tell us how vitalism, Schopenhauer, or the neo-Kantians have influenced his thought. In two important passages, however, he deals explicitly with epistemological questions. The first appears in *Psychological Types*, where he makes the famous distinction between those who know the world as object, such as Origen and Aristotle, and those who know the world as idea, such as Tertullian and Plato. In the extraverted and introverted types Jung sees the division between *esse in re* and *esse in intellectu*. He uses Kant's objections to the ontological argument to illustrate this division: Ideas may satisfy tests of rational coherence, but it is quite wrong to move from an idea to an assertion about objective reality. Jung states that psychology can mediate between the two extremes by combining outward things and inward understanding. In our psychological experience neither objects nor ideas have complete priority.

104 Ibid., 132-5.

105 Ibid., 257.

106 Ibid., 173.

Both come into play through the psychological process which Jung refers to as *esse in anima*. Nagy argues that this notion is not in fact a compromise position, but a triumph for the introverted type, a triumph in which Jung rejects the value-less nihilism of modern science in favor of subjective values: "(1) *Esse in anima* means to affirm inner values as over against either nominalist or purely rationalist views. (2) *Esse in anima* also means that reality itself equals the inner value of the subject. What is valuable is what is real."[107]

In later works, Jung also makes explicit reference to the 16th century alchemist and physician Paracelsus. Paracelsus understood knowing and the relation between self and world in terms of the "*lumen naturae*." He opposed the materialism and dogmatism of received medical authority; for while he agreed that the body consists of material elements, he thought that true cures did not come about merely through intervention at the chemical level. The body is not identical with its chemical composition. Its essence is rather to be found in its Archeus, its "inner principle of organization."[108] Paracelsus refused to rely on religious or medical authorities. He believed that one must discover what is true from facts illuminated by nature's own light as present in the soul.

Because we share being in common with the rest of nature, says Paracelsus, we know a thing by attuning our own being to its being–one principle of organization to another. In these acts of knowing, we gain self-knowledge and empirical knowledge at the same time. "We find that place in ourselves which is in sympathetic correspondence with the principle of the external object, and we know it because we know ourselves."[109] This theory of the *lumen naturae* presumably came to Paracelsus through the stoicized Neoplatonism common in Italy during the 16th century.

For Jung, the *lumen naturae* fits neatly into his theory of the unconscious psyche, whose darkness we illuminate through participation in the light of nature. In this borrowing from Paracelsus, Nagy finds further evidence for her thesis that Jung created a metaphysics of the psyche. All her arguments to this end imply that he therefore ended up in an indefensible position–an "idealist" belief system. Such metaphysical systems may have enjoyed a measure of intellectual respectability in the late 19th and early 20th centuries, the implication goes, but they no longer do. The materialists have won the great battle. Contemporary science does not allow for concepts such as teleology, as the downfall of the vitalist tradition demonstrates. Its surreptitious

---

[107] Ibid., 75-9.

[108] Ibid., 81.

[109] Ibid., 82.

introduction of metaphysical beliefs into empirical science was eventually exposed.

The Persistence of Metaphysical Questions

The modern consciousness of history has frequently relativized belief in closely held ideas. In Jung's period, traditional ideas about the nature of human beings and of God were undermined by historical consciousness and new scientific theories. Nietzsche claimed to have exposed Christian morality as the masked resentment of the weak towards those in power. Feuerbach explained God as an imagined Infinity created by psychological projection. The higher criticism of the Bible called into question the face value of biblical literature as evidence for Christian and Jewish claims about God and God's action in history. In biology, Darwin's theories appeared to explain the genesis of organisms through a process governed by chance, not divine intention.

These are a few of the critiques that Jung and other religiously committed individuals faced. Some of the critiques grew directly from critical history as a discipline, and all share a commitment to understanding reality as ultimately a matter of physical processes (and at most their epiphenomenal products) alone. The better our success in explaining the evolution of natural organisms, or the genesis of human moral sentiments, or the history and psychology of theological ideas, the less we need to appeal to occult, supernatural causes. At one time, this modern view surmises, we needed to appeal to transcendent causes to explain the world's existence; but now we know the world is the result of purely natural developments stretching out over a vast length of time. The quarrel over immanence and transcendence, nature and God, and science and religion becomes ever more irrelevant as modern scientific understanding pushes back the horizon of the well-explained further and further. Even if we occasionally appeal to transcendence as an explanation of anomalous phenomena, at heart our faith in science leads to the surety that a natural explanation will eventually replace all temporary intrusions of metaphysics and theology.

But I think we have reason to believe that coming to know the place of Jung's metaphysics in the history of philosophy and biology leaves the same metaphysical questions about the psyche that he faced unanswered. In a note at the end of her book, Nagy mentions the question of how to affirm inner experience after having discovered this place in history.

> [I have seen] concepts which once were able to contain all that I knew of the depth and mystery of human experience reduced to their place in a historical series.

> Strangely enough, my work as a Jungian analyst has not been affected, or only minimally so, although I feared that would happen. Reflection on why this might be so led me to the realization that nothing which is truly real can be changed by a merely ego-bound concept of it. What is real in the work I do seems to be, first, the symbolic process—the mystery of the dream and the sense of "meaningfulness" by which it is apprehended by the dreamer. Secondly, and above all, what is real is the human relationship in which maturity and highest value are sought. This is not affected by the language which may be used to describe experience, although we may be hard put to find language to indicate highest value in an age which has found God contrary to nature.
>
> It may be that neither the terms which have traditionally been used in Western philosophical/theological thought nor the analogous terms which Jung used in his psychology will survive encounter with the facts that life in the modern world entails. We must beware of a subjectivistic epistemology which obtains unity in mental perspective at the cost of denial of the facts by which we after all live in the world of time and space. Yet I believe that we may joyfully affirm the reality of inner experience, even if none of the terms presently available in the structure of language seems a suitable vehicle of that experience.[110]

In this view metaphysics and theology—"God-talk" in Nagy's phrasing—serve as vehicles to communicate inner experiences of highest value. These vehicles may not survive, however, and whether or not we will find new terms to communicate the reality of inner experience remains unclear. The practical core of Jung's teaching aligns very well with Kant's second critique and holds to the primacy of inner reality. But eventually Jung developed a system whereby inner values depend on discredited metaphysical ideas. He sided with the idealists, and this choice leaves him open to serious criticism in an age that does not find metaphysics and theology tenable.

Nagy's historical study of Jung's philosophical sources is unmatched in the literature on Jung. This study leads to fundamental questions that she has not set out to address other than historically. If what happens in the analytical relationship and the symbolic processes which accompany it does not fundamentally change when we abandon Jung's "metaphysical idealism," we must ask why it does not change. Perhaps his philosophical assumptions fall short; but if his psychotherapeutic methods do in fact accurately account for symbolic processes that take place in a person's development, then I think we must begin with the hypothesis that something about the psyche's reality grounds this accurate account. In other words, despite Jung's philosophical weaknesses, and despite the modern suspicion towards "metaphysics," we must continue to ask in what manner the psyche exists. To my mind, this is a

---

[110] Ibid., 269.

metaphysical question, if by metaphysical we simply mean a question about being, about what is. Yes, we do have to drop an essentialist metaphysics which suggests that psychic realities such as archetypes exist as immutable entities entirely untouched by the organic and historical developments of our world. But simply reverting to value language would do no good whatever in our quest for answers to questions about the reality of the psyche and its symbolic processes. These too exist as a real part of the world in which we find ourselves. A world whose reality both the old idealism and the old materialism fail to understand adequately.

In fact, the dawn of psychodynamic psychology had brought about a great challenge to exclusively materialist notions of reality. The discovery and elaboration of psychogenic causes for mental disorder demanded a more appropriate method than the materialism, mechanism, and determinism of the 19th century could provide. Bernard Lonergan makes note of this problem in *Insight* and places it in the context of the decline of the materialist world view:

> There is a final point to be made, and it regards the significance for depth psychology of recent developments in scientific methodology. At the turn of the century mechanist determinism was still the world view dominant in scientific circles. Freud's discovery and development of the notion of psychogenic disorder came at the ambiguous moment when the old outlook was about to dissolve, and as one might expect, the ambiguity of the moment forced ambiguity upon the interpretation of his work. Were mechanist determinism correct, then neither normality nor disorder could be psychogenic; Laplace's demon could calculate both from the world distribution of atoms in any basic situation; Freud could be said to introduce a new name and a new technique inasmuch as he dealt with collocations of atoms through their psychic appearances; but Freud could not be credited with the discovery of an autonomous science. On the other hand, if mechanist determinism is incorrect, the category of the psychogenic promptly assumes a profound significance.
>
> ... Again, Freud was professedly determinist. But insofar as determinism is operative in Freud's work, it amounts to the postulate that there is a reason for everything, even for numbers that one appears to select at random. But if one admits that some reasons are nonsystematic, that postulate becomes compatible with statistical laws; and if Laplace has failed to exclude probability from physics, there is little likelihood of its being excluded from psychology.... On the other hand, it is Freud's discovery that reveals the psychogenic to be more than an illusory name; and it is a sacrifice of mechanist determinism that opens the way to the recognition of the psychogenic as a genuine category.[111]

---

[111] *Insight*, 228-9.

Lonergan is showing the importance to psychology of the downfall of mechanist determinism in the natural sciences. What occurs in human beings at the level of psyche—whether ordering or disordering for mental health—has as much claim to reality as do the physical, chemical, and biological foundations of human existence. Further, these foundations do not provide sufficient explanations of what occurs at the psychic level. I think that the continued influence of materialism prevents intelligent recognition of this fact. Its dogmas are the presuppositions of the age, as J.J. Clarke reminds us.[112] Eric Voegelin writes that since the 19th century, metaphysics has been a word of abuse. From then on "the methods of science as the sole forms to study the contents of the world are declared to be the generally obligatory basis of man's attitude toward the world."[113] This is the implicit assumption of Rieff.

One of the ways that the level of psyche exercises its formative presence in human life is through symbolic presentations of image and story that mediate affective states to conscious awareness. These mediations can bring about a psychogenically based organization in the person. Lionel Corbett understands archetypal structures in a similar way—"independent of brain in terms of their own organization, and indeed ... responsible for the organization of the brain."[114] Such a statement does not necessarily entail an essentialist metaphysics or a reification of archetypes. On the other hand, it does require us to understand the reality of the psychic level as in some sense spiritual—that is, immaterial—since the physical and biological sciences do not provide full explanations for what occurs at the level of psyche.

I will work with the assumption that depth psychology in the late 19th and early 20th centuries did not have the philosophical tools with which to appropriate its own re-discovery of the psychogenic. It is clear that Jung rejected mechanistic determinism and looked for alternatives. His alternatives did not always succeed philosophically. Apart from my brief comments in the paragraphs above, I will not give further argument that we cannot reduce the psyche to its material foundations. Instead, I will move my argument forward by focusing on the benefit of a hermeneutical approach in the practical work of understanding the psyche's symbolic function.

---

[112] J.J. Clarke, *In Search of Jung: Historical and Philosophical Enquiries* (New York: Routledge, 1992), 100.

[113] Eric Voegelin, "The Political Religions" in *Modernity without Restraint*, ed. Manfred Henningsen, *The Collected Works of Eric Voegelin*, v. 5 (Columbia: University of Missouri Press, 2000), 60.

[114] Corbett, 58.

Hermeneutics and Jung's Psychology

Anyone who bases theoretical assertions on clinical experience must remember Stekel's famous dictum that patients dream in the dialect of the psychotherapist who happens to be treating them. Many dreams, interpretations, symptoms, emotions, and other psychological facts arise in an analyst-analysand relationship. Yet these data are very strongly particular to the two individuals and arise in an unusual context that is determined by conscious and unconscious factors, many of which neither party will ever explicitly advert to. Though such data do not easily ground generalizations, Jung appeals to clinical experience as a basis for archetypal theory. But if a patient brings a dream into the consulting room, tells it to the analyst, and the two wonder about its meaning for an hour, we can abstract no universal psychological principles from the event. What has the deepest significance in what has occurred derives not from the generalizable aspects of the event, but from the particularities of an interaction whose complexity largely escapes both participants. If the analyst is bright, however, he or she will have developed certain heuristic practices based on a career of experiencing similar occasions. For instance, the analyst will know that if a patient is acting over-confidently in general, and then a dream of falling from a great height occurs, it is often appropriate to interpret the dream as a warning against an inflated attitude.

J.J. Clarke notes Jung's own realization that his psychology belongs to the hermeneutical tradition. Jung never refers to Dilthey in the *Collected Works*, yet Clarke finds Dilthey's distinction between natural and human sciences useful for understanding Jung:

> In his later works he [Jung] drew a sharp contrast between "knowledge" and "understanding", seeing the former as the province of the physical sciences with their need to generalize, and the latter pertaining to the unique individual and to the unique products of individual cultures (US, p.7). It is, Jung accepted, possible to group individuals and the symbolic products of individuals into categories for the sake of making comparisons and analogies—a factor in historical studies fully recognized by Dilthey also—but without implying that this can lead to general laws from which predictions can be made.[115]

James Heisig makes a similar argument. Though he overemphasizes the role of rational insight in psychotherapy by neglecting the fact that symbol often mediates affective depth more effectively than reason does, he finally

---

[115] Clarke, 42-46.

concludes that Jung would benefit more from hermeneutical than natural scientific method:

> To take this ambiguity as essential to Jung's project is to suggest that we look at his psychology as primarily an abstraction from a therapeutic technique rather than as a scientific theory of mind for which supporting evidence could be found in psychotherapy. It is to hold Jung rigorously to his often-repeated assertion that his psychology had grown solely and exclusively out of his practice. It enables us to give better account, in my view, of the built-in limitations of Jung's work without gainsaying its brilliance or wide-reaching appeal....
>
> The defining characteristic of Jung's psychology of religion is his method of "objective amplification," which involves three stages: (1) the gathering of the primary data; (2) the search for parallels, analogies, and comparative material among the documents of history; and (3) the interpretation of the former in the light of the latter.[116]

Analytical psychology, argues Heisig, is not a natural but a human science. Its theory of the psyche is "metaphorical" rather than scientific, but this is quite acceptable for a human science. The archetypes of the wise old man, the great mother, and the divine child are not empirically verifiable entities. They are metaphorical images in a unique communication between analyst and analysand. Reference to analogous images from myth and folklore amplifies the therapeutic context by transposing it into a larger horizon of meaning. I would add, however, that our inability so far to verify rigorously that archetypes exist does not prove their non-existence. We may not yet have found an appropriate method with which to study them.

The Re-Discovery of the Psychogenic

Having found warrant through a philosophical evaluation to acknowledge the irreducible reality of the psychic level and attend to that level in practice by applying hermeneutical methods, I must now shift gears in order to demonstrate that the history of psychiatry—in addition to philosophy—supports my move in this direction. In his now classic work, *The Discovery of the Unconscious: The History and Evolution of Dynamic Psychiatry*, Henri Ellenberger chronicles the emergence of the psychogenic in psychiatry as a genuine category. The psychogenic has always been a controversial topic, but its study and clinical use has persisted in various forms:

---

[116] Heisig, 142.

> No branch of knowledge has undergone so many metamorphoses as dynamic psychiatry: from primitive healing to magnetism, magnetism to hypnotism, hypnotism to psychoanalysis and the newer dynamic schools. Furthermore, these various trends have gone through repeated waves of rejection and acceptance. However, acceptance has never been as unequivocal as in the case of physical, chemical, or physiological discoveries, not to mention the fact that the newer dynamic schools are to a great extent mutually incompatible.[117]

Strikingly, materialism intertwined itself with modern psychogenic-based therapies at the latter's beginnings. Franz Anton Mesmer (born 1734) played a key role in the development of dynamic psychiatry. The term mesmerism is coined from his name. Mesmer called his quasi-hypnotic therapy "animal magnetism." He cured his first patient, Fräulein Oesterlin, of fifteen severe symptoms by attaching magnets to her body, at which point she "began to feel extraordinary streams of a mysterious fluid running downward through her body, and all her evils were swept away for several hours." Mesmer did not believe that the magnets alone caused this remarkable event; instead, he theorized that the magnets helped to concentrate and direct a fluid in his own body through the patient. He called this transfer animal magnetism. If we are to trust Mesmer's account of the cure, it seems clear that he treated the illness psychologically by hypnotism and suggestion mediated through symbolic objects (the magnets) and his own powerful presence. In keeping with the imagination of the time, he understood the action of cure in crudely materialistic images.[118]

Mesmer popularized a modern method of psychogenic therapy. He and his followers eventually fell into disrepute, but others re-discovered similar treatments. The neurologist Jean-Martin Charcot turned his attention to psychology later in his academic career. In 1884-1885, experimentation led him to differentiate organic from hysterical paralyses. He went on to investigate the relationship between psychogenic paralyses brought about by hysteria, trauma, and hypnotic suggestion. Through hypnosis he produced paralyses identical to those found in patients who had lost the use of their arms with no organic cause after suffering a trauma. He reasoned that after the traumatic event a spontaneous hypnotic state must have occurred in these trauma victims. In 1892 he also differentiated between dynamic and organic

---

[117] Henri F. Ellenberger, *The Discovery of the Unconscious: The History and Evolution of Dynamic Psychiatry* (New York: Basic Books, 1970), v.

[118] Ibid., 59, 62-3.

amnesia. In the first, the patient could recover memories; in the second, re or she could not.[119]

Most theories and treatments that focused on the psychogenic arose outside the medical establishment.[120] Pierre Janet made the dramatic discovery that even apart from cases of hysteria, fixed subconscious ideas can bring about psychological disorder and physical symptoms. He recounted the case of Maria, whose blindness of the left eye he cured through hypnotherapy. He traced the blindness back to an early memory associated with her left eye. The memory itself had disappeared from awareness, but it still existed in a manner real enough to cause the symptom of blindness.[121] This symptom functioned symbolically; it made the unknown and unremembered idea known by representing it in the body. Janet found similar symbolizations in religious experience. His interest in religion led to a long relationship with Madeleine, a patient first admitted to the Salpêtrière in 1896. She wrote almost daily to Janet for many years and called him *mon Père*, though she also had a spiritual director. Madeleine experienced religious visions and endured many emotional and physical sufferings related to her spiritual identity. Skin lesions corresponding to stigmata were observed on her hands, feet, and the left side of her thorax during a stay at Janet's clinic.[122]

Janet's differentiated view of the genesis of such psychogenic manifestations sets him apart from many of his contemporaries. In Ellenberger's words,

> Janet's concept of neuroses belongs neither to the purely organicist nor to the purely psychogenic theories. In hysteria as well as in psychasthenia, he distinguished a psychogenetic process deriving from life events and fixed ideas and an organic substratum, that is, a neurotic predisposition.[123]

Janet turned to a concept from the physical sciences in his psychological theory: energy. He distinguished between the basic psychic energy that was discharged in an action, which he called psychological force, and the individual's ability to modulate this force, which he called psychological tension.[124]

---

[119] Ibid., 90-1.

[120] It is not surprising that the rebellious figure of Paracelsus became a hero for Jung, since both found themselves under suspicion for belief in immaterial realities.

[121] Ellenberger, 364.

[122] Ibid., 395.

[123] Ibid., 377.

[124] Ibid., 378.

When Charcot and others lent respectability to the trend, more scientists paid attention to the psychogenic. Ellenberger dates the period of "the first dynamic psychiatry" from 1775-1900. This movement had several common features: hypnotism as the method of choice; a focus on certain disorders, such as somnambulism, lethargy, catalepsy, multiple personality, and hysteria; a dual or plural understanding of consciousness that recognized "subpersonalities underlying the conscious personality"; and theories relating the etiologies of psychiatric disorders to the activity of "mental energy."[125]

Dynamic psychology challenged naively unitive views of human personality. Theories of dual and multiple personality—dipsychism and polypsychism—did not simply explain pathological states. They also forced a reassessment of the supposed unity of normal consciousness:

> One cannot overemphasize the influence that these two models of the mind, dipsychism and polypsychism, exerted on the systems of the new dynamic psychiatry. Dipsychism in its closed variety was the model from which Janet drew his concept of the subconscious and Freud his first concept of the unconscious as being the sum total of repressed memories and tendencies. Jung's theory of the unconscious was soon of the open variety, in that the individual unconscious is open to the collective unconscious of the archetypes. Both Freud and Jung evolved from a dipsychical to a polypsychical model of the human personality. With Freud, this occurred when he replaced his former model of the conscious-unconscious with his later three-fold model of the ego-id-superego, whereas Jung evolved a still more complex system.[126]

Both Charcot and Janet described how an idea could exist below the threshold of consciousness and gather a cluster of emotions and symptoms around itself. Jung later took up this notion in his theory of complexes, fragments of mental organization that develop outside our conscious control.[127] As Corbett shows, the unconscious for Jung contains complexes that function as independent centers of initiative. On account of this fact, "there is no hard and fast difference between consciousness and the unconscious, or at least the difference is ambiguous in his writing."[128] The polypsychical model is still relevant today, given similar notions in more recent psychoanalytic thinkers,

[125] Ibid., 110-11.
[126] Ibid., 147.
[127] Ibid., 149.
[128] Corbett, 114.

including Winnicott and Berne,[129] and in the literature of dissociation theory.[130]

Ellenberger has shown that—contrary to Rieff—we cannot understand the rise of dynamic psychology as essentially a Romantic revolt against the rationalism of the Enlightenment. Mesmer, for example, considered himself a son of the Enlightenment. History shows an interplay between figures such as Mesmer and Janet, both devoted to Enlightenment values, and Freud and Jung, whom Ellenberger considers "late epigones of Romanticism."[131] Even insofar as Jung is identifiably Romanticist, this identification does not exempt us from trying to understand his work on its own terms.

Certain aspects of Romanticism come through clearly in Jung—for instance, its quest for the ultimate ground of reality: "Behind the visible nature, the Romantic sought to penetrate the secrets of nature's 'fundament' (*Grund*), which he considered to be at the same time the fundament of his own soul. The means to reach that fundament not only lay in the intellect but also in the *Gemüt*, that is, the most intimate quality of emotional life." In reaction to this speculative quest, positivism rejected unknowable, ultimate realities in favor of demonstrable, visible facts. It was optimistic towards science and aggressive in applying technology for the material improvement of human life.[132] In contrast, Romantic feeling flared again in the voice of Nietzsche, who had a tremendous influence at the turn of the century.

Ellenberger rightly acknowledges the connection between Nietzsche and the developing "new dynamic psychiatry":

> An entire generation was permeated with Nietzschean thinking—whatever interpretation was given to it—in the same way as the former generation had been under the spell of Darwinism. It is also impossible to overestimate Nietzsche's influence on dynamic psychiatry. More so even than Bachofen, Nietzsche may be considered the common source of Freud, Adler, and Jung.[133]

Ellenberger traces various concepts of depth psychology to Nietzsche and his work of unmasking the brute instincts lying underneath culture and morality, a work that the psychologists undertook in their quest for the unconscious

---

129 Andrew Samuels, "Jung's Return from Banishment," *The Psychoanalytic Review*, 83:4 (1996): 469-490.

130 For example, see David Spiegel, ed., *Dissociation: Culture, Mind, and Body* (Washington, D.C.: American Psychiatric Press, 1994).

131 Ellenberger, 197-9.

132 Ibid., 200, 225-227.

133 Ibid., 276.

determinants of behavior. Though Freud made little explicit reference to Nietzsche, the similarities are clear; and Jung devoted an entire, multi-year seminar to the exegesis of *Thus Spake Zarathustra.*

The Nietzschean influence is certain, but we must remember that in the rest of his book Ellenberger establishes the experimental credentials of depth psychology. Where Nietzsche suspected that the will to truth was inimical to life and spoke out against scientism and historicism, the depth psychologists were engaged in scientific experimentation into the nature of the unconscious psyche. The influence of Nietzsche on Jung is especially confusing. Surely Jung's teleological understanding of human beings separates him from the great hermeneut of suspicion. I find it likely that Nietzsche held Jung's attention because of what the two shared in common: both were intellectually gifted pastor's sons who lost their Christian faith and suffered descents into near-psychotic depressions. Jung mentions the parallel in his autobiography, where he says that familial and professional obligations kept him sane during his dark night of the soul, whereas Nietzsche ultimately did not find his way back from his descent. As mentioned already, Jung's psychiatric position at the Burghölzli Mental Hospital under Eugene Bleuler served as a stern warning against romanticizing the unconscious.[134] Despite his obvious fascination with the dream world, Jung considers the order of consciousness an achievement; and he recommends the unmasking hermeneutics of suspicion only for the sake of further conscious development.

Towards a More Adequate Understanding of the Psychogenic

Jung's foundations in experimental psychology begin most clearly during his work at the Burghölzli. History credits Eugene Bleuler for replacing the term dementia praecox with "schizophrenia." He moved psychiatry away from the dominant and purely organicist understanding of this illness, favoring instead a theory that took account of both organic and psychogenic causes. He believed that the "primary" symptoms are caused by an unknown biochemical abnormality in the brain and that the "secondary" symptoms derive from the primary symptoms as well as psychogenic determinants. In other words, the primary "loosening of the tension of associations" is evidence of an organic

[134] Gerhard Wehr, *Jung: A Biography*, trans. David M. Weeks (Shambhala: Boston, 1987), 78-81.

dysfunction; and the secondary fantasies and splits in psychic functioning are symptoms that develop in interdependence with the loosened associative function and psychological factors.[135]

The unusual care and interest which Bleuler and his staff provided for the psychological life of patients reflects this differentiated view of causation in mental illness. Unlike the majority of asylums at that time, the Burghölzli extensively used one-on-one conversations between doctor and patient, work assignments, and other psychological and social interventions, always with the intent of establishing a stronger link to concrete reality. We see many of Jung's later therapeutic emphases prefigured here and may assume that the environment fueled his speculative interests as well. In the fantasies and hallucinations of patients Jung found parallels to the symbolic imagery of myth and folklore and began to posit the existence of a collective aspect of the psyche.

Jung's published work from this time consists mostly of experimental studies. Bleuler had given him responsibility for researching word association tests, and he took up this task with remarkable success. Ziehen had discovered that certain stimulus words provoked longer response times; furthermore, in some subjects these longer response times correlated with sets of words that shared an idea or an association with each other. It was often possible to move from these groupings to a further correlation with a traumatic memory, complicated relationship, or other emotionally charged aspect of the subject's life. Jung took these hypotheses and garnered evidence and further insights in tests with a large number of subjects. He found experimental verification of the polypsychical view, in particular of Pierre Janet's notion that subconscious fixed ideas exist as split-off psychic fragments.[136]

Jung called these fragments complexes. Though it is a long way from Jung's theory of complexes to his later speculations, he had found proof that the level of psyche was its own irreducible reality. This proof came in the form of statistically significant variances in expected response times. The experiments captured correlations of data indicating the remarkable role that meaning has in the organizational structure of the psyche. A range of words relating to the idea of theft, for instance, might provoke longer response times in a subject who is suffering from a guilt complex over having stolen money from his employer. That such a complex could provoke longer response times as well as a measurable galvanic skin response must have made a strong

---

[135] Ellenberger, 287.

[136] Ibid., 692.

impression on Jung and solidified his objections to materialism in psychology. Our contemporary lie detector tests grew out of these and other experiments. As Ellenberger notes, "The traditional speculative approach, which was also that of the Romantics, was now supplemented by two other approaches, the experimental and the clinical."[137]

In a more recent book, historian Sonu Shamdasani points out Jung's claim to include these other approaches by founding his psychology (in part) on the findings of French psychopathology. Shamdasani points out that the scientific perspective which Jung brings to the subject matter distinguishes his interest in visionary experience from that of "theosophical-gnostic sects."[138] The religious cultist wants to become unconsciously absorbed in the mysteries, whereas Jung interprets visionary data without falling into either obscurantism or over-confident rationalism.[139]

The Methodological Problems Facing Depth Psychology

Notions of psychic "energy" appear in Jung and Freud as well as Janet. The discovery of the psychogenic had advanced psychology beyond the materialism of the organicists, but the quasi-materialistic notion of energy remained. James Heisig argues that this problematic remnant stems from the fact that depth psychological method "in general still lumbers along in its covered-wagon days."[140] For instance, Jung uses symbolic images to explain psychological phenomena even when the most complex philosophical problems stand in the background. His imagistic style of writing creates unfortunate problems from the standpoint of the need for a cogent method on which to base his work. Heisig links the characteristics of this style with Jung's implicit methodology,

---

137 Ibid., 312.

138 Sonu Shamdasani, *Cult Fictions: C.G. Jung and the Founding of Analytical Psychology* (New York: Routledge, 1998), 83. For a survey of issues surrounding the experimental research of Jungian theories, see Mary Ann Mattoon, *Jungian Psychology in Perspective* (New York: The Free Press, 1981), 277-284.

139 Eugene Taylor also emphasizes Jung's reliance on the French dynamic psychologists as well as on William James and F.W.H. Myers. Eugene Taylor, "The New Jung Scholarship," *The Psychoanalytic Review*, 83:4 (1996): 547-568.

140 James W. Heisig, *Imago Dei: A Study of C.G. Jung's Psychology of Religion* (Lewisburg: Bucknell University Press, 1979), 103.

clues to which he finds in various sections of the *Collected Works*. According to Heisig, Jung rightly rejected the old mechanistic-materialistic concepts of causality but did not provide a well-thought out alternative. Yet clearly he wants to appreciate Jung's accomplishment in a sympathetic way: "if the genius of Jung's work is to be properly located and given its due place in the history of psychology, an alternative methodological groundwork to his own is essential." He divides Jung's own methodological statements into three categories: the "primacy of experience," a "quasi-Kantian subjectivism," and a defense of the "energic point of view."[141]

Jung claims to use a "phenomenological" method. By this he simply means an overriding preference for experiential facts over theoretical assumptions.[142] He considered Freud overly attached to his theory of the sex drive and lauded William James as a man unfettered by excessive theoretical bias.[143] His frequent claim to be an "empiricist" or "phenomenologist" translates into an appeal to the primacy of psychological experiences as present in our immediate experience. Heisig points out that unfortunately, immediate "experience" rarely speaks for itself. It requires mediation through the activities of memory, reflection, etc.

I have already written extensively of Jung's "quasi-Kantian subjectivism." Heisig argues that he pays little attention to the intricacies of Kant's critical philosophy and instead relies in a very general way on Kant to support the claim that we know our immediate psychic experiences and only them. There are no Archimedean points from which to judge the psyche. In addition to the structures of cognition, Jung believes that archetypal structures in the unconscious also determine what and how we know that which exists outside the psyche.[144]

In Heisig's view, Jung tries to escape the subjectivist implications of his neo-Kantianism by proposing an "energic point of view":

> As a check against the opposing tendencies to naïve realism and transcendental idealism that we have seen in his empiricism and his subjectivism, Jung was forced to recognize that in some sense fact and theory are correlative concepts, incomprehensible without one another.[145]

---

[141] Ibid., 110-11.

[142] Ibid., 111.

[143] He makes this statement after he and Freud visited Clark University in Massachusetts. Wehr, 122-3.

[144] Heisig, 113-14.

[145] Ibid., 114.

He recognizes two modes of reflection, the "genetic-causal-mechanistic" and the "synthetic-final-energic." Since both are strictly "regulative" principles according to Jung's neo-Kantianism—not inherent properties of things-in-themselves—he feels justified in applying both and insisting that mechanistic causes are no more real than final causes. The synthetic view led to the theory of synchronicity, which Heisig understands as Jung's attempt to justify the fact that his psychology has "dispense[d] with the principle of causality" and thereby freed itself from "the demands of natural science for experimental verification through prediction."[146] According to this theory, coincidental occurrences happen completely by chance from the genetic-causal-mechanistic view, but sometimes connect meaningfully from the synthetic-final-energic view. Heisig finds it odd that Jung describes synchronicity as an "acausal connecting principle." Unfortunately, if synchronicity is truly acausal, it tells us nothing beyond the meaning that we impute to coincidences. Once it tries to say more, it becomes a causal principle, though more akin to final than efficient cause. Heisig would have preferred a straightforward affirmation of final causality as the right explanation for synchronistic events.[147]

Concluding Remarks

In this chapter, I have dealt with several levels of questions regarding Jung's theoretical underpinnings: his relation to the history of philosophy, the history of biology, the hermeneutics of symbolic experience, and the history of psychiatry and rise of depth psychology. I will be focusing in my remaining chapters on symbol formation from the practical, hermeneutical standpoint. Heisig argues that Jungian language generally works for patients in analysis and that a hermeneutical understanding takes account of that fact without embroiling us in Jung's philosophical problems. I will analyze the way in which Jung believes that symbols mediate the unconscious psyche to consciousness. In order to understand this mediation, I will turn for help to Lawrence's work as described in Chapter 1.

---

[146] Ibid., 116.

[147] Ibid., 120. Having made this criticism, I add that a more careful examination of the primary texts on synchronicity might show that Jung in fact does come to a more adequate notion of causality. Some scientists have argued that advances in quantum field theory make synchronicity more plausible as a theory. For example, see Victor Mansfield, *Synchronicity, Science, and Soul-Making* (Chicago: Open Court, 1995).

Finally, I would like to warn against trying to understand Jung as simply the product of sources that influenced him. No single one of these influences adequately sums up his central concern. The question at the heart of Jung's entire work is the question of the *psyche's reality*. He was convinced of this reality, and his use of various sources shows a search for support of this conviction. The resulting mix of original and derived ideas constitutes a complicated and sometimes inconsistent attempt to relate the reality of the psyche to various fields. On account of the modern split between materialism and idealism, science and religion, fact and value, Jung's affirmation of the psyche's reality and opposition to the mechanistic world view come across as an endorsement of what Nagy calls "metaphysical idealism." That moniker tends to neglect Jung's roots in French psychopathology and the far-reaching implications of its re-discovery of the psychogenic. It also neglects the possibility that Jung was trying to push beyond the limitations of the materialist–idealist debate in which he was caught, but could not find the means to achieve a more adequate grounding.

▪ CHAPTER FOUR ▪

The Symbolic Life

In chapter 1, I examined Rieff's polemical arguments against Jung and in doing so discovered some of the questions that surround the controversial intersection of religion and depth psychology. In chapter 2, I explored the historical influences on Jung from philosophy and psychology and found that unlike many modern thinkers, he rejects the idea that religion will disappear as human consciousness achieves ever-greater scientific understanding of the world. The psyche has a "religious function" that will remain a part of human reality indefinitely, quite apart from the fate of the traditional Western religions. Despite the many criticisms made of Jung, both deserved and undeserved, he consistently brings our attention to this religious function that modernity has often neglected.

Not every modern psychologist has given religion short shrift. In French dynamic psychiatry and its re-discovery of the psychogenic, Jung found support for his study of the psyche's inherent religiousness. The influence of the French school pre-dated his collaboration with Freud and contributed to the grounds on which he diverged from Freud's system. On the philosophical front, neo-Kantian subjectivism also opened the way for investigating religion as a natural function. In an age dominated by mechanistic materialism, this subjectivism undermined the materialist's claim to possess the sole methods for adequately understanding all reality. It called into question *both* claims about the psyche *and* claims about physical entities, since in neither case do we have access to things-in-themselves. Despite the philosophical shortcomings of this subjectivism, the materialism of that age had its own shortcomings and would potentially have bracketed out the whole of psychic reality, not simply the religious function. Jung's subjectivism had at least this advantage: he was able to follow a post-Kantian "turn to the subject" in the realm of depth psychology and give a sophisticated description of the psyche.[148] I will focus from this point forward on Jung's contribution to the phenomenology and hermeneutics of symbols and the role they play in the development of the individual person.[149]

My inquiry into Jung's phenomenology of symbol formation will concentrate on early works from 1912 through 1935. First, I will begin with a 1929 commentary that he wrote on a Chinese meditation text. This commentary highlights Jung's desire to recover a contemplative style of discipline for use in psychological practice. He examines the discipline of attaining a "still point" in consciousness and identifies the meditative symbols in the Chinese text as symbols of the "self." Second, I will turn to the beginnings of Jung's notion of practicing "the symbolic life"—moving from a 1912 account of "The Two Kinds of Thinking" to a 1916 account of practical methods for facilitating symbol production. Third, I will summarize a series of important definitions from the 1921 edition of *Psychological Types*. Finally, I will conclude with a summation and an example of the symbolic life taken from Jung's "Tavistock Lectures" of 1935.

Before I move on, please recall a crucial point from chapter 1. Frederick Lawrence opposed Richard Rorty's "sceptical derailment of hermeneutics" by arguing that Gadamer in fact reintroduced the question of truth by insisting on the priority of concrete performances. By keeping our attention on the concrete performances of living, we also stay close to the relevant questions of truth. To reiterate:

> The practical or political question has to do with judging the way one makes sense of one's life. This is the mother-lode or matrix of hermeneutic philosophy's recovery of the truth-question both from epistemology and from technical and scientistic dominance. *Wahrheit und Methode* shows how creating or appreciating a work of art, writing history or carrying out any scholarly investigation are not separated from the finite acts, attitudes, and orientations by which I take up a direction for my life.... A direction in life or a way of life is true, to the degree that it contributes to one's

---

148 Robert Doran writes of Jung's "turn to the subject" in his essay, "Jung and Catholic Theology," in *Catholicism and Jungian Psychology*, ed. J. Marvin Spiegelman (Phoenix, AZ: Falcon Press, 1988), 42-3.

149 I will use the terms "phenomenology" and "hermeneutics" quite generally to mean, respectively, the descriptive investigation of symbolic phenomena and the practice of interpreting such symbols.

excellence or, as we would say today, one's genuine development and authentic selfhood.[150]

In the case of Aristotle's practical syllogism, the relevant performances consist in "apprehending an end, consenting to it, deliberating concerning means, and choice of the means." In the case of Jung's practical psychology, I suggest that the relevant performances consist in attending to, imaginatively expressing, and interpreting symbols that arise in the psyche. Such work is intimately linked to taking up a direction for one's life. The individual engaged in a symbolic experience always does so in a life inseparably tied to questions and choices regarding ends—particularly, for Jung, to those that pertain to "genuine development and authentic selfhood."

Lawrence is primarily interested in the higher order functions of reflection and decision rather than the affectively conditioned world of symbols. But symbols effectively bring the inchoate world of unconscious affect into relationship with conscious reflection and choice. And Jung does not see goal-directedness as *solely* the business of conscious intentions (of the "ego," in his terminology). He also finds it—though in less developed form—in symbolic dreams and fantasies. Paradoxically, he says, the symbols that contribute to living out one's proper end emerge more readily when the individual temporarily suspends the usual intentionality of ego-functioning. To show this in depth, I now turn to his phenomenology of symbol formation, which he explains in a number of important essays.

The "Realism of the East"

Jung's emphasis on the concrete comes across most clearly when he writes about Asian religions and the psychology that informs them. They are rich traditions of practical wisdom centered on the human subject, a "realism of the East." This realism regards the feelings, thoughts, and sensory life of the subject as its primary concern, as opposed to the predominant realism of the West, whose primary concern is the world of objects known by the natural sciences. Though he chastised Western groups which mimicked Asian practices without attending to their own historical roots, Jung hoped that the West could revitalize its own traditions of subject-oriented, contemplative practice. He writes hopefully of the West's eventually developing its own

[150] Lawrence, 19-20.

"yoga," its own meditative disciplines, and reaching a sophisticated level of differentiation in this introverted area to match that of Asia.

The evidence shows that for a non-specialist, Jung had been reading quite widely outside the Western tradition since at least the years prior to 1921. In the Tavistock Lectures (1935), he refers to the psychological insights he gained from this work:

> We Europeans are not the only people on the earth. We are just a peninsula of Asia, and on that continent there are old civilizations where people have trained their minds in introspective psychology for thousands of years, whereas we began with our psychology not even yesterday but only this morning. These people have an insight that is simply fabulous, and I had to study Eastern things to understand certain facts of the unconscious.[151]

In fact, many references to Vedic hymns, the Upanishads, and various Buddhist and Taoist texts occur in *Psychological Types* (1921)[152] as well as several shorter essays and introductions.[153] In the late 1920s, sinologist Richard Wilhelm sent his friend Jung a German translation of *The Secret of the Golden Flower*, an 18th century Chinese manuscript containing instructions on meditation. Jung wrote a psychological commentary to accompany its publication. According to Wilhelm, the manuscript almost certainly derives from an older text and originally existed as a centuries-old oral tradition. Its ideas are found in the T'ang period of the 8th century A.D. in a sect called the "Religion of the Golden Elixir of Life."[154] The sect undertook a revival of classic Taoist philosophy.

---

[151] C.G. Jung, "The Tavistock Lectures," in *The Symbolic Life: Miscellaneous Writings*, v. 18, trans. R.F.C. Hull, in *The Collected Works of* C.G. *Jung*, ed. Herbert Reed, Michael Fordham, and Gerhard Adler, exec. ed. William McGuire, Bollingen Series XX (Princeton: Princeton University Press, 1989), § 139.

[152] C.G. Jung, *Psychological Types: Or, The Psychology of Individuation*, trans. H. Godwin Baynes, (London: Routledge and Kegan Paul, 1923), 242ff.

[153] For example, Jung's "Psychological Commentary on *The Tibetan Book of the Great Liberation*," "Yoga and the West," "Foreward to Suzuki's *Introduction to Zen Buddhism*," and "The Psychology of Eastern Meditation," in *Psychology and Religion: West and East*, v. 11, trans. R.F.C. Hull, 2nd ed., in *The Collected Works of* C.G. *Jung*, ed. Herbert Reed, Michael Fordham, and Gerhard Adler, exec. ed. William McGuire, Bollingen Series XX (Princeton: Princeton University Press, 1969), §§ 74-8.

[154] Richard Wilhelm, trans. and ed., *The Secret of the Golden Flower: A Chinese Book of Life*, commentary by C.G. Jung (New York: Harcourt Brace & Company, 1962), 5-6.

Both Taoist and Buddhist influences show through strongly in *The Golden Flower*. Briefly put, this text instructs the pupil in a contemplative discipline whereby the meditator discovers a stable point in consciousness. This stable point is identified with the Tao, the undivided unity beyond the world of finite things, and makes possible a transformed relationship to the world of change. Jung's commentary first appeared in Wilhelm's 1929 edition of the text. The commentary is particularly interesting, because in it he outlines a psychological understanding of "the symbolic life" as a form of contemplative discipline analogous to that which the text describes. He also gives an important early definition of the self as a symbol of transcendence. Whether or not Jung has interpreted the ancient text accurately, what he says makes an excellent starting point from which to examine his analysis of symbol formation.

The Secret of the Golden Flower "begins with the ultimate insight he [the author] has set out to attain"—namely, the nature of the Tao—"that which exists through itself [and] is called the Way."[155] Jung notes that such a beginning leads directly into the vexed question of transcendent reality, but he keeps his focus on questions of practice. Striving for the Tao demands a detachment from the world of objects nearly inconceivable to the modern Westerner. Meditation brings about freedom from attachment, or aversion. Consciousness does not become entangled with anything; neither does it exclude anything. It rests in stillness, noticing all the psychic contents that arise—images, sensations, thoughts, emotions—yet not moving from its place at the still point by pursuing what arises. The intentional ego, on the other hand, does make such pursuits. It focuses attention through concentration and is therefore able to carry an intention through to its conclusion. In our text, however, the only goal is to remain at the point of stillness and cultivate a non-reactive attention:

> The pupil is taught to concentrate on the light of the inmost region and, while doing so, to free himself from all outer and inner entanglements. His life-impulse is guided towards a consciousness without content which none the less permits all contents to exist.[156]

Like the transcendent Tao, the pupil becomes free from entanglement in the world of change but is nevertheless present for all that exists.

There is nothing unusual here to the literature of instruction on meditation. "Consciousness without content which none the less permits all

[155] Ibid., 97.

[156] Ibid., 122.

contents to exist" describes quite well the goal of certain traditions of Buddhist meditation. The unitive nature of this consciousness consists in its allowing *all* that arises in the psyche to exist. The appropriate image to accompany meditation is the mandala, which facilitates the state that it symbolizes. A mandala is simply a circle that usually contains four (and sometimes more) sections and a variety of images within its circumference. The contents often represent opposites—light and dark, heaven and earth, compassionate deities and fierce deities, etc. These opposites emphasize the circle's ability to contain even disparate elements. Like the Tao, it transcends multiplicity. The Golden Flower belongs to this common class of symbols that appear so often in the religious iconography of both East and West. According to Jung, it symbolizes the totality of the psyche, a reality that one only comes to know imperfectly through practicing a discipline such as that outlined in the Chinese text.

The Symbol of the Self

So far Jung has taught the basic shape of the consciousness that pupils must seek. They cultivate it through meditative discipline, withdraw attention from objects and focus on attaining a still point, suspend the normal functioning of the intentional ego, allow subjective mental states to arise and pass away, and attend to these without becoming entangled in them. The consciousness attained is identified as the Tao and symbolized by the mandala of the Golden Flower. In Jung's own words,

> This description of fulfillment pictures a psychic state which perhaps can best be characterized as a detachment of consciousness from the world, and a withdrawal of it to an extra-mundane point, so to speak. Thus consciousness is at the same time empty and not empty. It is no longer preoccupied with the images of things but merely contains them. The fullness of the world which heretofore pressed upon consciousness has lost none of its richness and beauty, but it no longer dominates consciousness. The magical claim of things has ceased because the original interweaving of consciousness with the world has come to an end. The unconscious is no longer projected, and so the primal *participation mystique* with things is abolished. Therefore consciousness is no longer preoccupied with compulsive intentions but turns into contemplative vision, as the Chinese text very aptly says.[157]

Jung takes these meditative themes and transposes them into his own depth psychology and its terms—the unconscious, the ego, the self, and the

[157] Ibid., 122-3.

developmental process that an individual person undergoes. The presence of symbols provides the key link between present-day psychological work and the ancient text. What so excited Jung when he read Wilhelm's translation was his recognition that symbols very much like the Golden Flower had appeared in his own inner life and in the dreams and artistic expressions of his patients:

> As has already been pointed out, the union of opposites on a higher level of consciousness is not a rational thing, nor is it a matter of will; it is a psychic process of development which expresses itself in symbols. Historically, this process has always been represented in symbols, and to-day the development of individual personality still presents itself in symbolical figures.[158]

The mandala appeared to function especially well both as an aid to the development of consciousness and as the spontaneous product of its achievement.

Jung did not want to be labeled a "mystic." Yet his how-to description of living a life attentive to symbolic reality does in fact describe a form of contemplative practice. Consider, for example, his description of the self and the way it emerges in psychological work. In his commentary, Jung gave his first full description of this symbol as a unifying factor, a superordinate source of order for the totality of the psyche. Living a life rooted in the self sounds very close to a contemplative liberation of consciousness:

> But if the unconscious can be recognized as a co-determining quantity along with the conscious, and if we can live in such a way that conscious and unconscious, or instinctive demands, are given recognition as far as possible, the centre of gravity of the total personality shifts its position. It ceases to be in the ego, which is merely the centre of consciousness, and instead is located in a hypothetical point between the conscious and the unconscious, which might be called the self. If such a transposition succeeds, it results in doing away with *participation mystique*, and a personality develops that suffers only in the lower stories, so to speak, but in the upper stories is singularly detached from painful as well as joyful events.
>
> The creation and birth of this superior personality is what is meant by our text when it speaks of the holy fruit; the "diamond body", or refers in other ways to an indestructible body.[159]

A change in consciousness thus causes a true change in the human person. Desire for such a change is not a desire to escape the world. Rather, it flows from a need to forge a new relationship to the world of change and suffering,

---

[158] Ibid., 99.

[159] Ibid., 124.

so that one can give oneself over completely to the task of living.[160] In Jung's view, contemplative disciplines originate in "an atmosphere of suffering, seeking, and striving common to all civilized peoples; it is the tremendous experiment of becoming conscious, which nature has laid upon mankind, and which unites the most diverse cultures in a common task."[161] Seeking the "holy fruit" calls on a potentiality that Jung says exists—or so we may assume—in embryonic form in everyone.[162]

In the years following his commentary, Jung made the self an increasingly important component of his psychology. It appeared in the first version of *Psychological Types* (1921) in an early form. Jung appears to have solidified the notion only after he had studied Asian religious practices and perceived in them a confirmation of his own growing understanding of how the psyche shifts its organizational structure to include the self. I will now turn to the development of Jung's understanding of the symbolic process that goes along with this shift—the "transcendent function," as he refers to this process in an early essay.

The "Two Kinds of Thinking"

Jung wrote his commentary on *The Golden Flower* in 1929. He claims that the text confirmed what he had discovered for himself. I have suggested that the influence of Asian religion was substantive as well as confirmatory. But it remains true that these discoveries grew from his own practice of psychotherapy. In addition, he like Freud carried out an intensive self-analysis. Professionally, the years following the break with Freud in 1913 were years of relative isolation for Jung. He became very depressed and immersed in his own inner life. But his most seminal ideas emerged after this time, including those concerned with symbol production and its role in the individual's psychological development. Clearly, he formed these ideas on the basis of several factors: his own symbolic experiences, those of patients, and what he learned from a variety of written sources.

Yet Jung was laying the groundwork for a practical psychology of the symbolic life even earlier than the break with Freud. In 1912, he published his first major book, *Wandlungen und Symbole der Libido*. At this point Jung still

---

160 Ibid., 95.

161 Ibid., 136.

162 Ibid., 92.

followed Freud in several essential ways. Through the dream, an "intellectual image" enters awareness and obeys "wholly other laws and purposes" than does consciousness. What lies behind the imagery are the desires for the coming day. He cites the instance of a common motif, the sexual assault, often represented by an attack with a lance, dagger, or other object signifying a penis. The motif communicates the repressed "lust and anxiety" in the dreamer. Jung expresses this Freudian point in blatantly teleological terms:

> Dreams are symbolic *in order that* they cannot be understood; *in order that* the wish, which is the source of the dream, may remain unknown.[163] [italics mine]

His preference for thinking mythologically as well as teleologically also seems clear. When he writes that ancient people considered dreams to be communications from a deity, he does so with a distinct tone of approval for the spirit though not the letter of this belief.

The early section, entitled "Two Kinds of Thinking," lays the groundwork for later developments in Jung's view of symbol production. Without the directive involvement of intentionality, the flow of consciousness takes on a dreamlike quality, which Jung calls *fantasy thinking*, the first of the two kinds of thinking.[164] Consistent with his phylogenetic standpoint, he associates fantasy with both childhood and primitive cultures. It is an early mode of consciousness in the history of the human race. The conscious life of ancient people was generally characterized by a high degree of fantasy, he argues. It resembled quite closely the dream and its associative, imagistic, affect-laden structure. In the experience of the child and the myth-making primitive, the individual does not exist as a being who is clearly differentiated from the world. Both project the psyche's associations and affects onto objects in the external world. Here Jung uses Levy-Bruhl's idea of *participation mystique* to indicate the state of identity between the primitive and his or her world. In the modern adult, dreams show us that a significant measure of this primitive/childhood identity is still operative in the flow of affect-charged images.[165]

Moderns, however, largely outgrow *participation mystique* and fantasy-thinking as the primary mode of being. They graduate to what Jung calls

---

[163] C.G. Jung, *Psychology of the Unconscious: A Study of the Transformations and Symbolisms of the Libido, A Contribution to the History of the Evolution of Thought*, trans. Beatrice M. Hinkle, 1916 (New York: Dodd, Mead, and Company, 1949), 12.

[164] Ibid., 25.

[165] Ibid., 27.

directed thinking, the second of the two kinds of thinking. This mode is distinct from fantasy largely on account of its ability to concentrate attention in an intentional way. Words take on the role of signs that stand for things in the world, and the thinker mirrors causal sequences of events in the world with corresponding sequences of thoughts. Because it enables us to adapt to the environment and to communicate with others, directed thinking has teleological implications.[166] Without it civilization would not exist. For the primitive and the child, words are attached in a very concrete sense to objects in the world. They are essentially identical with objects. Thus the primitive often uses the word as a magical device to control the object; he who possesses the name of a thing possesses the thing. But directed thinking can occur only when one abstracts the word from the concrete object. Only then is it possible to understand causal sequences of events, apprehend desirable ends, develop strategies to bring those ends about, and bring the inward processes of the psyche into the awareness and partial control of a conscious ego. The ego is then able to communicate its experiences in a way that others also understand. For this reason, directed thinking underlies the formation of social bonds that are based on conscious understanding.[167]

When word and object, self and world, and self and other are differentiated, humanity and culture develop and libido becomes "mobile"—that is, transferable to ends other than the instinctual drives of sex, hunger, and aggression. It becomes differentiated from pure instinct. Combined with our ability to think intentionally, the differentiated libido has made it possible for human beings, a physically vulnerable species, to secure their place in the world and create civilizations.

The human struggle to civilize the world is characterized by effort and exhaustion, whereas fantasy seems to expend no energy:

> Whoever attentively observes himself will find the general custom of speech very striking, for almost every day we can see for ourselves how, when falling asleep, phantasies are woven into our dreams, so that between the dreams of the day and night there is not so great a difference. Thus we have two forms of thinking—*directed thinking* and *dream or phantasy thinking*. The first, working for communication with speech elements, is troublesome and exhausting; the latter, on the contrary, goes on without trouble, working spontaneously, so to speak, with reminiscences. The first creates innovations, adaptations, imitates reality and seeks to act upon it. The latter,

---

[166] Ibid., 16.

[167] Ibid., 17.

> on the contrary, turns away from reality, sets free subjective wishes, and is, in regard to adaptation, wholly unproductive.[168]

While this early view of fantasy thinking appears quite negative, even here Jung shows signs that he wants to redeem fantasy thinking as humanly valuable and not necessarily maladaptive. The first sign is his explanation of the less attractive consequences of directed thinking. To create modern civilization and its sciences, "the modern culture-creating mind is incessantly occupied in stripping off all subjectivity from experience."[169] In other words, it strips away the vestiges of *participation mystique*, in which subjective factors are mixed in with objects. But some level of connection between subject and world seems to make the world a meaningful, habitable place, says Jung. Without it the world feels dead. In general, however, he believes that modernity has not fully eliminated the archaic *participation mystique*.[170] When the exhausting concentration required for directed thinking flags, the threshold separating consciousness and the unconscious weakens and affect-charged fantasies again come streaming into our awareness. As of 1912, Jung emphasized the real as the adaptive, the differentiated, and the egoic, though he began to explore the adaptive potential of fantasy thinking. In subsequent writings, however, he explicitly acknowledges a larger horizon of human meaning that allows for the essential importance of non-directed thinking. He came to believe that in addition to the civilizing order that directed thinking brings about, another form of order—symbolic order—also plays an indispensable role in human life.

"The Transcendent Function"

By 1916, six years after he first wrote of the "Two Kinds of Thinking" and about twelve years before his commentary on *The Golden Flower*, Jung had made significant developments in his phenomenology of symbol formation in the individual's life. In that year, he wrote "The Transcendent Function," an essay that did not see publication until 1957, when it was rediscovered in Jung's files and included in slightly revised form in the *Collected Works*. It describes the technique for facilitating symbol formation that Jung later called the technique of active imagination. Already in 1916, this practice had

[168] Ibid., 22.
[169] Ibid., 24.
[170] Ibid., 31-6.

developed to the point that he was able to write, though not to publish, a coherent account of its use that amounts to bringing fantasy thinking into a productive relationship with consciousness.

Jung gave an abbreviated account of the practice in his commentary on *The Golden Flower*, where he writes of the symbol as the "new thing" that arises in consciousness and mediates between the affective and the rational levels. But the as-yet-unpublished essay on the transcendent function gives a fuller account of this process. It is a particularly popular essay, in part because many find Jung's tendency to reify his theoretical notions less pronounced at this early stage.[171] He seems less prone to mislead the reader by speaking of the realities of psychic functioning—complexes, symbols, etc.—as things that exist apart from the psychic functioning itself.

To put it another way, he stays close to the questions of concrete performance. In the 1950 preface to "The Transcendent Function," it is quite clear that Jung's study of Asian religions influenced the essay. He states that this first attempt "at a synthetic view of the psychic process in analytical treatment " is concerned with a problem that is

> identical with the universal question: How does one come to terms in practice with the unconscious?
>
> This is the question posed by the philosophy of India, and particularly by Buddhism and Zen. Indirectly, it is the fundamental question, in practice, of all religions and all philosophies. For the unconscious is not this thing or that; it is the Unknown as it immediately affects us.[172]

Jung's own answer to this universal question is to show how the symbol—the "new thing," to use the terms of the *Golden Flower* commentary—is created, and

---

[171] The papers from the twelfth International Congress for Analytical Psychology in 1992 attest to this popularity. They are published in Mary Ann Mattoon (ed.), *The Transcendent Function: Individual and Collective Aspects* (Einsiedeln, Switzerland: Diamon Verlag, 1993).

[172] C.G. Jung, "The Transcendent Function" ([1916]/1957), in *The Structure and Dynamics of the Psyche*, v. 8, trans. R.F.C. Hull and Gerhard Adler, in *The Collected Works of C.G. Jung*, ed. Herbert Reed, Michael Fordham, and Gerhard Adler, exec. ed. William McGuire, Bollingen Series XX (Princeton: Princeton University Press, 1970), §§ 67-8. This bold statement reminds us that for all the supposed care he took to stay within the boundaries of psychology, Jung was perfectly capable of making far-reaching statements about religion.

how this creation reflects a new mode of relating to the unconscious. The transcendent function brings about the mediating symbol, and to understand this function we must begin with several *basic terms* from the essay:

- There is a metaphorical *threshold* dividing the conscious and the unconscious psyche. For a content—an image or an emotion, for instance—to cross the threshold and enter awareness, it must possess intensity. If too weak, it will remain unconscious. Many contents exist in a latent fashion below the threshold. We can legitimately speak of such "unconscious contents," because in symptoms, dreams, hypnotic states, and the like, we sometimes discern their presence.
- We exclude what is incompatible with the focus of our concentration through *inhibition*. The strength of the conscious attitude is roughly consonant with the ability to inhibit the influx of fantasy thinking and concentrate our attention through directed thinking. To use the more common word, repression plays a necessary part in mental life.
- Organized groupings of what lies below the conscious threshold are called *fantasies*. If their intensity is strong enough, or the tension at the threshold is weak enough, they stream into consciousness.
- A *compensatory* relationship exists between consciousness and the unconscious:

> Experience in analytical psychology has amply shown that the conscious and the unconscious seldom agree as to their contents and their tendencies. This lack of parallelism is not just accidental or purposeless, but is due to the fact that the unconscious behaves in a compensatory or complementary manner towards the conscious.[173]

A successful, adaptive conscious attitude requires directed thinking, which requires inhibition of the fantasy elements. These must stay below the threshold, for they are

> likely to bias the intended direction to suit their purpose and so lead to an undesired goal. But how do we know that the concurrent psychic material is "incompatible"? We know it by an act of judgment which determines the direction and path that is chosen and desired. This judgment is partial and prejudiced since it chooses one particular possibility at the cost of all the others. This judgment in its turn is always based on experience, i.e., on what is already known. As a rule it is never based on what is new, what is still unknown, and what under certain conditions might

---

[173] Ibid., § 132.

> considerably enrich the directed processes. It is evident that it cannot be, for the very reason that the unconscious contents are excluded from consciousness.[174]

The development of consciousness beyond a merely passive flow of psychic contents therefore involves one-sidedness as a matter of course. This one-sidedness cannot be helped. An individual distracted by powerful fantasies could never concentrate attention on thinking through and accomplishing worthwhile goals. Yet this necessary one-sidedness sparks a compensatory reaction from the unconscious. Inhibition does not eliminate what lies below the threshold. Given enough energy, these contents burst onto the conscious scene as symptoms, slips of the tongue, dreams, or other unconsciously conditioned events.[175] If the attempts to compensate fail, the unconscious complexes may gain further intensity and cause a neurosis. In a neurosis the complexes have overtaken the personality.

Even a neurosis therefore has a compensatory meaning in Jung's psychology. It signals the need to pay attention to and find a workable relationship with the disturbing influence of the unconscious. What Jung wants is a way to maintain the adaptive strength of the conscious attitude while remaining open to the fantasies that arise. "The unknown" and "the unconscious" are essentially negative terms. They describe what we do not know and are thus illimitable. Jung chastises the belief that psychoanalysis can eventually empty an individual's unconscious. The ego will never be the unchallenged master of its own house, because consciousness and the unconscious only make sense as two terms of psychodynamic activity. The tension between them never disappears, and we never find a final reconciliation: "Adaptation is never achieved once and for all.... Man needs difficulties; they are necessary for health."[176]

From Signs to Symbols

The illimitable nature of the unconscious and its unending tension with the conscious attitude signal the need for a different psychotherapeutic goal. For Jung, the goal is to develop a symbolic attitude, that is, a new way to exist in relation to the unconscious through the active appropriation of its symbols:

---

174 Ibid., § 136.

175 Ibid., § 138.

176 Ibid., § 143.

> The basic question for the therapist is not how to get rid of the momentary difficulty, but how future difficulties may be successfully countered. The question is this: what kind of mental and moral attitude is it necessary to have towards disturbing influences of the unconscious, and how can it be conveyed to the patient?[177]

This goal demands the inclusion of both poles: consciousness and its directed thinking, and the unconscious and its fantasies. This combination appears impossible by definition, since opposites are precisely that—opposite. If we become explicitly aware of something unconscious, we say it has become conscious and the opposition immediately dissolves. But Jung proposes a third pole, the transcendent function. It mediates between the first two without turning the unconscious content into something explicitly known.[178] This pole implies that it makes sense to speak of a kind of "knowing" which is not clear and distinct, rational knowing, but which nevertheless amounts to more than simple unconsciousness. The "transcendence" of this function simply indicates its mediating position between two seemingly irreconcilable positions, not something "mysterious or metaphysical."[179]

Central to this mediating function is the individual's longing for a new way of bringing order to the psyche which has been disturbed by intrusions that it cannot integrate. This longing expresses itself in the relationship with the analyst, to whom the patient "clings" out of hope for a much-needed "renewal of attitude." The so-called "transference" in the analytic relationship has a true, forward-looking purpose, namely, to make apparent and carry out the longing for a new adaptation. It involves more than simply projecting parental images onto the analyst.[180]

The same concern for developmental direction shows itself in Jung's method of interpretation, by which he asks what dreams or fantasies mean in relation to a person's developmental needs. While a dream may have more than one valid interpretation, asking forward-looking questions brings it into a new context where developmental goals become quite relevant to the interpretation. The compensations to the conscious attitude tend to illuminate what the psyche needs to adjust itself. Not that Jung thinks the psyche always heals its own difficulties, but in his view a general tendency towards readjustment does exist. His hermeneutics is therefore anti-reductive. Discovering underlying early memories and repressed wishes helps to

---

177 Ibid., § 144.

178 Ibid., § 145.

179 Ibid., § 131.

180 Ibid., § 146.

understand the unconscious material retrospectively, but one must look forward as well.

This appeal to *telos* has struck critics as metaphysical and therefore unscientific. Yet it does not in fact claim that some pre-existing Form of a person's destiny lies behind the unconscious material. Rather, it makes sense in relation to a theory of symbol that Jung espoused *after* having written *Wandlungen und Symbole der Libido*:

> The method is based, rather, on evaluating the symbol (i.e., the dream-image or fantasy) not *semiotically*, as a sign for elementary instinctual processes, but symbolically in the true sense, the word "symbol" being taken to mean the best possible expression for a complex fact not yet clearly apprehended by consciousness. Through reductive analysis of this expression nothing is gained but a clearer view of the elements originally composing it, and though I would not deny that increased insight into these elements may have its advantages, it nevertheless bypasses the question of purpose. Dissolution of the symbol at this stage of analysis is therefore a mistake.[181]

In 1912 Jung had not yet distinguished "symbols" from "signs." Both terms denoted what he now means in this passage by "signs." This important shift in definitions derives from his new conviction that it is possible to redeem fantasy thinking. The transcendent function and its symbolic mode of communication constitute this bringing of the unconscious fantasy level into relation with the conscious personality and its adaptive goals.

The Practice of the Transcendent Function

Now that several of the terms are defined, I turn to the actual phenomenology of the transcendent function—how it functions and what one can do to facilitate it. First, one needs unconscious material, which Jung divides into dreams, symptoms of unconscious complexes, and spontaneous fantasies. Strictly speaking, none of these are unconscious once we are aware of them. But they do originate from psychic activity below the threshold, and that is the important fact. Dreams are generally "unsuitable or difficult to make use of in developing the transcendent function, because they make too great demands on the subject."[182] Spontaneous fantasies tend to possess the highest degree of coherence and are Jung's favorite material with which to induce the transcendent function. Since one produces fantasies while awake (though in a

[181] Ibid., § 148.

[182] Ibid., § 153.

state of lessened tension at the threshold of consciousness), they tend to be less cryptic. A practical method is helpful in coming to terms with these fantasies. Jung outlines the usual stages of the practice that he has used for this purpose.[183]

First, the need for a new attitude often comes about because of a disturbance. Unconscious contents invade consciousness. At that point, Jung recommends attending to the disturbance with an allowing awareness worthy of any meditator:

> He must make himself as conscious as possible of the mood he is in, sinking himself in it without reserve and noting down on paper all the fantasies and other associations that came up.... This work by itself can have a favourable and vitalizing influence. At all events, it creates a new situation, since the previously unrelated affect has become a more or less clear and articulate idea, thanks to the assistance and co-operation of the conscious mind. This is the beginning of the transcendent function, i.e. of the collaboration of conscious and unconscious data.[184]

This stage suspends the normal activities of directed thinking and centers attention on elaborating an image or fantasy through drawing, painting, imaginary dialogue, sculpting, or other expressive media. The individual withdraws attention from the world of objects, does not push away or hold onto anything that arises, and in this way discovers the affect around which the images and associations orbit. The affective state achieves some clarity, since the expressive work brings affects out of their inchoate state and puts them in a symbolic form.[185] The compensating factor has then found a symbolic order through which consciousness is able to appropriate it.

Jung sees two ways to elaborate the fantasy material further. Each way has dangers if taken to the extreme. First, "creative formulation" develops the symbolic material into stereotyped symbols. One then feels connected to a wider horizon of archetypal images, but the danger comes when one feels overly impressed with the aesthetic merit of the product. This pitfall would mistakenly shift attention away from the affective value for the subject; and without the affect, the process of development would come to a stop. Second, the way of "interpretation" tries to understand the product's meaning in rational terms. Here as well the danger comes when attention is diverted from the subject's affective response. A one-sided focus on interpretation might try to bring the material completely into the light of understanding. But

---

[183] Ibid., § 155.

[184] Ibid., § 167.

[185] Ibid., § 170.

disturbing influxes from the unconscious will always trouble the conscious attitude; we cannot expect to fathom all this material rationally now or in the future. It may not even be desirable to do so. The affective component of experience can be of great value. Jung thus hopes to cultivate a mode of being conscious that does not evade the "meaning and value for the subject."[186]

After the discovery phase just described, the focus shifts back to the conscious attitude, which must now come to terms with what has arisen: "This is the second and more important stage of the procedure, the bringing together of opposites for the production of a third: the transcendent function. At this stage it is no longer the unconscious that takes the lead but the ego."[187] If the ego did not step in at this point, the fantasies would be merely passive. They would sweep through the subject, who would receive no benefit from them. By its very nature an affect has the effect of weakening the conscious function. The primitivity of the affect makes it a dangerous intruder. Jung expresses the danger by referring to Pierre Janet's concept of the "*abaissement du niveau mental.*" When he originally borrowed this notion that conscious functioning breaks down when tension at the threshold lowers, he did so in order to explain the emotionality that colors thoughts which are associated with unconscious complexes. He had demonstrated this coloring in his word-association experiments. The transcendent function remedies this situation by giving symbolic expression to affects that persistently elude the ordering effect of intellect.

> The confrontation of the two positions generates a tension charged with energy and creates a living, third thing—not a logical stillbirth in accordance with the principle *tertium non datur* but a movement out of the suspension between opposites, a living birth that leads to a new level of being, a new situation.[188]

The symbol thus creates its own kind of order—not primarily one of rationality, but one that gives an affect meaning and value for the subject, thus harnessing the power of the emotional level for the good of a developing personality.

[186] Ibid., § 176.
[187] Ibid., § 181.
[188] Ibid., § 189.

Definitions from *Psychological Types* (1921)

We have seen the beginnings of what Jung came to term "active imagination" (c. 1935): first, the distinction between "two kinds of thinking" (1912) and, second, symbol production as a "transcendent" psychic function that mediates unconscious contents to consciousness (1916). In order to highlight active imagination as analogous to meditative practice, I began this chapter with a somewhat later work (*The Golden Flower*, 1928), in which for the first time Jung (a) gives an extended treatment of the relationship between psychological work and meditation/contemplation and (b) relates his idea of the "self" to such practices by explaining it as a source of symbolic order for the psyche. Though it does not contain his developed notion of the self, the original edition of *Psychological Types* (1921) lays down most of the basic terms of Jung's psychology. The lengthy section of definitions represents Jung at his most systematic. Since that word does not often apply to him, it is worthwhile to summarize a number of the relevant terms. All the writings subsequent to 1921 presume familiarity with these definitions.

Affect. A strong emotion, almost always involuntary, causing a physical innervation and a disturbance of the thinking process.[189]

Attitude. A "readiness of the psyche to act or react in a certain direction." In other words, a complex combination of psychological factors that amount to a propensity to understand and act on stimuli in a particular direction. For instance, any of Jung's four functions—thinking, feeling, intuition, or sensation—could become the habitual attitude of an individual. These and any other general groupings, however, do not negate the fact that attitude is essentially an individual phenomenon.[190]

Compensation. The self-regulating function of the psyche.[191] See the description in my previous section.

Consciousness. That which mediates psychic contents to the ego. We say that something is "conscious" or "in my consciousness" when "I" am aware of it in a definite way.[192]

Constructive. Equivalent to "synthetic" in Jung's vocabulary—that is, the method of interpreting unconscious products to discover the needed developmental change for the person and help carry it through. Jung opposes

189 *Psychological Types* (1923), 522-3.
190 Ibid., 526-30.
191 Ibid., 532-3.
192 Ibid., 535-6.

this term to the reductive method of interpretation, which discovers the historical or logically prior causes of the unconscious products.[193]

Differentiation. The separation of parts from a whole. In psychology, the developmental process in which psychic functioning divides into the relatively discrete functions of thinking, feeling, intuition, and sensation.[194]

Ego. The subject of conscious life. The one doing the directed thinking and intentional acting.[195] Ego and "self" constitute the fundamental polarity in the psyche, a polarity of conscious center to unconscious center.

Fantasy—Active or Passive. Passive fantasies, such as dreams, that occur to one without any effort, and active fantasies consciously fostered to express more meaningfully contents originating below the threshold.[196]

Feeling. The ego's subjective reaction of like or dislike, often involving an affective component but also capable of intentional, rational direction. Thus the highly developed "feeling function" for Jung is a "rational" function that makes judgments about whether something is good or bad.[197]

Identity. A state of sameness between subject and object often characterized as a pathological regression into unconsciousness. Identity might be the result of *participation mystique*.[198] As I will show in Chapter 4, a truly *symbolic* experience cannot occur if one exists in a state of identity.

Individuation. The development of a human being into a person aware of his or her distinctness from the group:

> In general, it is the process of forming and specializing the individual nature; in particular, it is the development of the psychological individual as a differentiated being from the general, collective psychology. Individuation, therefore, is a *process of differentiation*, having for its goal the development of the individual personality.[199]

According to Jung, individuation is inextricably tied to the transcendent function, "since it alone can provide that individual line of development which would be quite unattainable upon the ways dictated by the collective norm."[200]

---

[193] Ibid., 536-7.
[194] Ibid., 539-40.
[195] Ibid., 540.
[196] Ibid., 573-81.
[197] Ibid., 543-6.
[198] Ibid., 552-3.
[199] Ibid., 561.
[200] Ibid., 562.

Libido. Psychic energy, not necessarily sexual. Energy here means the subjective intensity of a psychological process.[201]

Participation mystique (taken from Lévy-Bruhl). A connection with the object that renders the subject unable to differentiate him or herself from it completely. A state of partial identity.[202] I will argue in Chapter 4 that symbolic life requires an ability to engage in states similar to *participation mystique* while simultaneously sustaining one's differentiation as a conscious subject.

Projection. The process by which a subjective state, such as an affect, is imparted to an object. Projection sometimes functions as a way of ridding oneself of an unwanted personal quality by seeing it as characteristic of another person. Yet it also holds the possibility of leading to self-knowledge; for once one becomes aware of the act of projecting, one is then able to claim the projected content as one's own.[203]

Symbol. When the transcendent function is activated, a mediating symbol may arise from the psyche's depth. What it mediates is the unknown—often an affectively powerful, unimagined, but potential future development of one's personality. In other words, it communicates the subject's own potential being to his or her conscious awareness. It symbolizes an as-yet-unrealized aspect of the person, one that may or may not actually come into existence in the form that the symbol points to. The symbol (a) is partly known and partly unknown; (b) cannot be fully explained in terms of known associations; (c) cannot be a symbol unless the subject apprehends it as a symbol;[204] and (d) is full of emotional meaning in a way that engages the subject and gives value to undifferentiated affects.[205]

Thinking—Active and Passive. Thinking differentiated according to the presence (active) or absence (passive) of the subject's intention. A reasonable thought could very well occur to one apart from actively pursuing it in a train of thought.[206] This definition shifts in Jung's later writing, where he prefers to speak of "directed thinking" and "fantasy thinking." It then becomes unclear where "passive" thoughts that are not unconscious fantasies fit into his scheme.

---

[201] Ibid., 571-2.

[202] Ibid., 572-3.

[203] Ibid., 584-5.

[204] He or she does not, for example, treat it as a mere sign.

[205] Ibid., 814-29.

[206] Ibid., 611-2.

Transcendent Function. The psychic process by which (a) directed thinking is suspended; (b) contents arise from the unconscious and are accepted into awareness; (c) an active elaboration of these contents takes place; and (d) a mediating symbol emerges that provides a way out of the oppositional standstill between the conscious attitude and the unconscious compensation.[207] I will spend a large portion of Chapter 4 analyzing this function and its potential theological importance.

Unconscious. Not a metaphysical entity, but "a psychological boundary-concept, which covers all those psychic contents or processes which are not conscious, *i.e. not related to the ego in a perceptible way*." The existence of such contents is known largely through the evidence of psychopathological cases, including those in which "the ego knows nothing of the existence of extensive psychological complexes, and in the next moment a simple hypnotic procedure is enough to bring the lost contents to complete reproduction."[208] Note that the lack of presence to the ego's awareness is the defining factor.

The Symbolic Attitude

Having traced the idea of the transcendent function as it developed from about 1912 through 1928, I then summarized the definitions from the 1921 edition of *Psychological Types* that are relevant to this idea. Now I am able to make a somewhat more systematic statement of what Jung means by the "symbolic life" or "symbolic attitude," and to add an example that he gave in his 1935 "Tavistock Lectures." Identifying the formal structure of the symbolic attitude and referring to a particular instance of its practice do little to communicate the subject's affective experience. Yet they do at least make Jung's view explicit enough that it can become a topic of conversation in this book.

First of all, the *symbol* mediates aspects of the psyche that are both known and unknown—for example, those nebulous emotions that have begun to dawn on a person but are too ineffable to be known more unambiguously. The symbol thus performs a heuristic function; it is "the best possible description, or formula, of a relatively unknown fact; a fact, however, which is none the less recognized or postulated as existing."[209] In the psychological

---

[207] Ibid., 610. Defined under "Symbol."
[208] Ibid., 613-5.
[209] Ibid., 601-3.

sphere, this unknown quality does not simply stem from a lack of data but relates to the fact that symbols express contents which are heavily conditioned by affects, and affects by their very nature cause an *abaissement du niveau mental*. It is in these terms that Jung asks his crucial question: How does one come to terms with the unconscious? In other words, how does one bring the nebulous formations of the unconscious into a constructive relationship with the rational, intentional direction of the conscious attitude?

When an image arises that is felt by the subject to capture the meaning for his or her life of the unconscious formation, then we can speak in Jung's terms of an authentic symbol. The subject experiences a feeling of resonance which indicates that the symbol has mediated the situation in the unconscious truthfully. This resonance is itself full of emotional significance for the subject, who cannot distance him- or herself from the symbol. It lives too close to the heart. Such closeness can act as an impediment when a strict differentiation between the subject and his or her object of investigation is required. When it comes to questions of living one's life authentically, however, the felt resonance of the symbol's truthful mediation is an essential aspect of a meaningful life. In Jung's view, we cannot even call something a symbol apart from the subject's involvement:

> Whether a thing is a symbol or not depends chiefly upon the attitude of the consciousness considering it; as for instance, a mind that regards the given fact not merely as such but also as an expression of the yet unknown. Hence it is quite possible for a man to produce a fact which does not appear in the least symbolic to himself, although profoundly so to another. The converse is also possible.[210]

The symbolic attitude "is only partially justified by the nature of things." It does not attend to the world simply for its own sake and on its own terms, as the natural sciences strive to do, but considers the world in its relation to the desires of the human heart. For this reason, the "world" of symbolic reality lies in between the world of things as they simply are and the world of our desires as they would be if we could separate them from the need to live our lives in relation to "the nature of things." But we do not and cannot live apart from this relation.

Descriptive phenomenology and hermeneutics have proved the better methods for understanding the symbolic attitude as Jung has formulated it—better than methods that purposefully eliminate the influence of the subject's affective life. A lengthy description of a particular case in which someone carried out the symbolic attitude is now called for. To illustrate what he means

---

[210] Ibid., 603.

by the change in attitude effected by symbolic work—that is, the shift of the subjective center from ego to self—Jung in his Tavistock lectures makes reference to a former patient:

> Moreover, this work has a definite effect on him [the patient]. Whatever he has put into it works back on him and produces a change of attitude which I tried to define by mentioning the non-ego centre.
>
> I will give you an interesting example. I had a case, a university man, a very one-sided intellectual. His unconscious had become troubled and activated; so it projected itself into other men who appeared to be his enemies, and he felt terribly lonely, because everybody seemed to be against him. Then he began to drink in order to forget his troubles, but he got exceedingly irritable and in these moods he began to quarrel with other men, and several times he had very disagreeable encounters, and once he was thrown out of a restaurant and got beaten up. And there were more incidents of that sort. Then things became really too thick for his endurance, and he came to me to ask my advice about what he should do. In that interview, I got a very definite impression of him: I saw that he was chock-full of archaic material.... I sent him to a woman doctor who was then just a beginner and who did not know much about archetypal material....
>
> She told him to watch his dreams, and he wrote them all down carefully, from the first to the last. I now have a series of about thirteen hundred dreams of his. They contain the most marvelous series of archetypal images. And quite naturally, without being told to do so, he began to draw a number of pictures which he saw in his dreams, because he felt them to be very important. And in this work on his dreams and on these pictures he did exactly the kind of work which other patients do by active imagination....
>
> In the course of this analysis, which took him through about the first four hundred dreams, he was not under my surveillance. After the first interview I did not see him at all for eight months. He was five months with that doctor, and then for three months he was doing the work all by himself, continuing the observation of his unconscious with minute accuracy. He was very gifted in this respect. In the end, for about two months, he had a number of interviews with me. But I did not have to explain much of the symbolism to him.
>
> The effect of this work with his unconscious was that he became a perfectly normal and reasonable person. He did not drink any more, he became completely adapted and in every respect completely normal. The reason for this is quite obvious: that man—he was not married—had lived in a very one-sided intellectual way, and naturally had certain desires and needs also. But he had no chance with women at all, because he had no differentiation of feeling whatsoever. So he made a fool of himself with women at once, and of course they had no patience with him. And he made himself very disagreeable to men, so he was frightfully lonely. But now he had found something that fascinated him; he had a new centre of interest. He soon discovered that his dreams pointed to something very meaningful, and so his whole intuitive and scientific interest was aroused. Instead of feeling like a lost sheep, he thought: "Ah,

> when I am through with my work in the evening, I go to my study, and then I shall see what happens. I will work over my dreams, and then I shall discover extraordinary things." And so it was. Of course his rational judgment would say that he just fell violently into his fantasies. But that was not the case at all. He did a real bit of hard work on his unconscious, and he worked out his images scientifically. When he came to me after his three months alone, he was already almost normal....[211]

In this illustration, we see the clear analogy between Jung's active imagination and the components of contemplative practice as he elaborated them in his commentary on *The Golden Flower*. These shared components include:

- An initial disturbance that defies the normal solutions of the intentional ego.
- The setting aside of time in which one withdraws attention from the outer world and cultivates a presence to oneself—a "still point" in the shifting flow of consciousness.
- Suspension of the ego's normal functioning, particularly its directed thinking.
- The practice of an allowing awareness that accepts into consciousness whatever arises.
- The appearance of symbolic concomitants to the above practice, particularly symbols of the hypothetical non-ego center, the self, and its ability to contain the full range of psychic experience. These symbols reinforce the process they reflect.
- Dissolution of the *participation mystique* that gives unconscious intrusions their compulsive quality. Paradoxically, by shifting one's attitude towards acceptance of such intrusions, the man is able to stop projecting them onto others and thus succeeds in reestablishing the differentiation of subject and object.
- The consequent return to the world of waking consciousness and normal relationships with others.
- Retrieval from this whole episode of what Jung refers to as the "holy fruit," that is, the ability to contain the unconscious by finding one's still point so as to imbue the world with new value for the subject, who has been able to bring the affects that arise into a state of higher, symbolic differentiation.

His new "centre of interest" turned out to be necessary for the man's development as a responsible individual in the world. By stepping back and

---

211 "Tavistock Lectures," §§ 402-5.

finding a non-ego source of psychic organization, he found that he was then able to contain the disagreeable affects that had been disturbing his relations with others. In other words, the symbolic work quickened his maturation as a person. Jung's Tavistock Lectures recall, in fact, Stanley Hall's definition of analysis as the quickening of the maturation process through psychotherapeutic treatment.

Concluding Remarks

The purpose of this third chapter has been to present the early development of Jung's method for facilitating symbol production—the "transcendent function" or "active imagination," which he spoke of more generally as integral to "the symbolic life" or "the symbolic attitude." I have found that Jung offers his idea of the symbolic attitude as an answer to what he considered a universal religious question, namely, the question of how to achieve a fruitful relationship with the unconscious. This relationship can be fruitful because symbols point to and encourage adaptive changes in personality. Their effect demonstrates the open structure of personal existence. Persons develop, and symbolic experience has a hand in this development. The prospective interpretation of symbols acts as psychotherapeutic midwife for this natural function. Jung found support for his own practical psychology in *The Golden Flower* and other Asian religious texts. He began to speak of a "realism of the East," its introspective and highly developed practical wisdom. The West, he argues, must stand on the ground of its own history and discover its own contemplative practices, its own yoga.

The symbolic life is clearly Jung's attempt to present a contemplative style of practice for the modern West. Asian religious ideas did not simply confirm his own discoveries in this area. They most likely cross-pollinated themselves into his thought and terminology. I traced the notion of the symbolic attitude and its basis in the transcendent function from "Two Kinds of Thinking," to the long-unpublished "The Transcendent Function," to the definitions in *Psychological Types*, and to the presentation of "active imagination" given in the lectures at Tavistock. Jung's later work presumes familiarity with this phenomenology of symbol formation. Many of his later works concern themselves with comparative material from the historical texts of alchemy, gnosticism, and world mythology. These fed into the theory of archetypes and of the collective unconscious, both of which I will largely neglect in this book. They involve other difficult problems regarding the ubiquity of certain symbols. Such problems grow out of the early work that I am focusing on, but for better or worse moved Jung to develop what is essentially a mytho-speculative system.

Instead, I will be focusing on whether the "symbolic life" as Jung presents it—and as I will develop it in Chapter 4—contains within its dynamics a movement towards contemplation of divine transcendence. After considering the areas of Jung's thought where readers usually identify "transcendence," my analysis will center not on these areas so much as on fleshing out the transcendent implications of his early work on the practices of symbolic life. I will focus especially on understanding the differentiation of a "still point" of conscious presence to the flow of symbolic formations. This focus will lead me to conclude that the still point's differentiation constitutes a matter of theological importance that readers of Jung and Jung himself have for the most part neglected.

• CHAPTER FIVE •

Transcendent Presence

Through an extended reflection on one of Jung's most strident critics, Philip Rieff, I began this book by identifying the division so often made between Jung the "religious" depth psychologist and his irreligious peers—those psychologists who stay faithful to the modern critique of transcendence. Jung and Freud are typically the key figures in this division: Jung the pseudo-scientist, the proponent of a psychological substitute for faith, and Freud the courageous atheist, the penultimate hermeneut of suspicion. Even though the appeal of this dichotomy lingers, a portion of contemporary Freudian thought has shed its suspicious, reductive attitude towards religion and recast itself in favor of subject-oriented hermeneutics, theories of intersubjectivity, and in some cases a surprising openness to blatantly mystical ideas. At the end of this last chapter, I will discuss the apparent closing of the divide between some Freudian psychoanalysts and Jung on questions of religion. But first I will continue my investigation of the symbolic function by asking whether—with or without Jung's own explicit acknowledgment or philosophical affirmation—it points beyond the horizon of finite existence towards divine reality.

Readers of Jung usually think of "self symbols" as the source of his work's transcendent implications. I will ask whether this impression is correct and analyze the self's function in detail. This analysis will lead to the natural conflicts between a psychology that analyzes projections and a theology that speaks of a divinity beyond projection. A recent article on the heated disputations between Jung and Martin Buber will prove helpful at this juncture. Though his theories do not meet the tests of "hard science," Jung did hold very strictly to an "empiricism" for which all that lies outside the psyche remains forever closed to psychological (or any other form of) investigation.

I will argue that Jung did not solve the subjectivist problem of the psyche's encapsulation within itself on the level of theory, but that in practice the symbolic life does lead beyond the psyche to a contemplation of divine transcendence. By analyzing this contemplative move I will develop a theology of the symbol-producing function. Understanding the "still point" of presence mentioned in *The Golden Flower* will prove central to my argument, which grows out of Jung's insights yet does not foreclose the theological horizon. For philosophical support I will briefly present Eric Voegelin's analysis of divine presence in human consciousness, a presence symbolized as the "Beyond." Based on my arguments up to this stage, I will then conclude that the still point in symbolic life engenders a movement of faith to contemplate the ordering divine presence that reveals itself in the soul.

From there I will go on to show that the emergence of "Jungian" ideas and questions of transcendence in contemporary psychoanalytic literature supports my position. After a short survey of this emergence I will analyze Thomas Ogden's essay on "Potential Space" as an example of the contemporary Freudians' strong interest in symbol formation. For Ogden the capacity to symbolize is essential to the creation of a human subject. I will find that Ogden, Michael Eigen, Wilfred Bion, and others show an awareness that unknown, irreducible, and perhaps transcendent factors operate in the symbolic life of a human subject. For instance, Eigen uses the Bionic notion of "faith in truth" in a way that resonates with Frederick Lawrence's identification for dialectics of a self-transcending intention to truth. Yet these psychoanalysts are only beginning to explicate the transcendent factors, and their favored language of "intersubjectivity" serves this explication only up to a point and then falters when faced with intimations of divine transcendence.

Having found that the formal structure of the symbolic function includes a potential for contemplation of transcendent presence, I will conclude the book with my final reflections on the theological importance of this contemplative movement and work several key insights from earlier chapters into the argument of chapter 4.

Alignment with the Self

As I have shown in Chapter 3, for Jung the symbol mediates affect to our conscious awareness. We typically regard affect as an expression of what is most primitive in us. Our instinctual drives erupt to the surface as affect. What then could such a function have to do with a contemplative ascent towards divine reality? My argument will proceed in four stages prior to the sections on Voegelin and on contemporary psychoanalysis. First, I will show that self symbols suggest but do not necessarily entail contemplation of divine transcendence. Second, I will discuss the problem of theology as projected anthropology and reiterate Jung's epistemological subjectivism as outlined in Chapter 2. Third, a section on Jung's disputations with Martin Buber will illustrate the subjectivist problem as it relates to theology. Fourth, I will turn to a symbol from Jung's essay on *The Golden Flower*—the symbol of the "still point"—and show that understanding this still point of conscious presence leads us to the true theological importance of Jung's work on symbol.

Chapter 3 focused on the "transcendent function." In Jung's eyes, the "transcendence" of this function has nothing to do with theology, but instead consists in its ability to mediate the unknown, unconscious psychic situation to our conscious awareness through the play of imaginative expression. My analysis showed that the literature of Eastern spiritual practice resonates for Jung with the symbolic processes that he discovered in the psychological development of individual persons. The text of *The Golden Flower* outlines stages that parallel these processes. To reiterate, the common elements consist in:

- An initial disturbance that defies the normal solutions of the intentional ego.
- The setting aside of time in which one withdraws attention from the outer world and cultivates a presence to oneself—a "still point" in the shifting flow of consciousness.
- Suspension of the ego's normal functioning, particularly its directed thinking.
- The practice of an allowing awareness that accepts into consciousness whatever arises.
- The appearance of symbolic concomitants to the above practice, particularly symbols of the hypothetical non-egoic center, the self, and its ability to contain the full range of psychic experience. These symbols reinforce the process that they reflect.
- Dissolution of the *participation mystique* that gives unconscious intrusions their compulsive quality. Paradoxically, by shifting one's attitude towards acceptance of such intrusions, one is able to stop projecting them onto others and thus succeeds in reestablishing the differentiation of subject and object.
- The consequent return to the world of waking consciousness and normal relationships with others.
- Retrieval from this whole episode of what Jung calls the "holy fruit," the ability to contain the unconscious by finding one's still point, so that the world is newly imbued with value for the subject, who has

> been able to bring the affects that arise into a state of higher, symbolic differentiation.

Readers of Jung typically point to the appearance of self symbols as the locus of transcendence in the symbolic life. Because they communicate the "whole," they seem to imply an infinity beyond human comprehension. Our inability to comprehend the totality of the psyche is permanent, since according to Jung the depth of the psyche has no predetermined bottom; and the production of dreams, fantasies, emotions, etc. continues throughout the life cycle to come up with new and often surprising contents. Self symbols communicate this infinite quality by presenting images that draw our attention to the psyche's vast depth and by symbolically containing that depth. In *The Golden Flower* both the Tao and the mandala perform this function.

Though "self" points beyond the horizon of everyday consciousness, it leads to no immediate theological conclusion. It may simply force us to expand our notion of human being to include the unconscious and its illimitable depth. On the other hand, Jung calls the self a "god-image" and recognizes that its numinosity plays an essential role in the human quest for God. But how do we think about this God? As a wholly immanent content of the psyche? Or as some other sort of reality? I will be carrying this question through to the end of the chapter.

In *The Golden Flower*, symbols of the self arise when the meditator achieves contentless consciousness and becomes aware that what there is to be conscious of extends far beyond the normal boundaries of ego-functioning. This discovery creates the need for a symbol to communicate the vastness of the new horizon. In other words, symbols such as "Tao" arise because the meditator has ascended to an awareness that transcends the normal horizons of consciousness. Jung does not spell out this ascent adequately. Instead, he characterizes symbolic life and meditative discipline as quests to align one's conscious attitude with the psyche's unconscious depth. The practitioner is *descending* into the unconscious, not *ascending* to a new kind of consciousness.

In Jung's view, the task of practice is to align oneself with the unconscious depth. For him no once-and-for-all "analyzed" person ever exists. There is only the person who succeeds or fails to align the ego with the depth. It cannot conquer the depth; nor should it try, since emotional meaning requires the affect that originates in the unconscious. Successful alignment occurs through a symbolic process in which one appropriates the self symbols that arise and thus aligns ego (the conscious attitude) with self (the "center" at the depth of the whole psyche). To understand this alignment I summarize what Jung says about self symbols and their function. First, they express a detachment that results in the discovery of a non-egoic center: "All we can say rationally about this condition of detachment is to define it as a sort of centre within the psyche of the individual, but not within the ego. It is a non-ego center."[212] Second, self symbols express the entirety of the psyche, so that the mandala—the penultimate visual symbol of an encompassing whole—is for Jung a self symbol.[213] Third, they express an order in the psyche that originates outside conscious awareness: at its deepest level the unconscious is characterized by "a concentric or radial order which constitutes the true centre or essence of the collective unconscious."[214] Fourth, self symbols presage and encourage the psychological development of the individual. They create a connection to inner resources that provide solutions to psychological problems. An urge to become what one is originates in the depth of the psyche.[215] Jung's notion of the self thus expresses two distinct mysteries: first, the mystery of the whole, the sense of a totality beyond the ego's horizon; and, second, the mystery of an ordering "center" discovered within this whole.

Jung identifies a final goal of alignment between the ego and this self that is both whole and center. In his interpretation the meditator in *The Golden Flower* works to achieve liberation from bondage to objects in the world. He speaks of the same liberation in the "Tavistock Lectures" and connects it to the goals of psychotherapy. Detachment from the world of objects creates "the diamond body," a stage in which one no longer projects inner life onto outer things and by this withdrawing of projections dissolves the primitive *participation mystique* between subject and object:

> I call this *fourth stage* of the therapy of transference the *objectivation of impersonal images*. It is an essential part of the process of individuation. Its goal is to detach consciousness from the object so that the individual no longer places the guarantee of his happiness, or of his life even, in factors outside himself, whether they be persons, ideas, or circumstances, but comes to realize that everything depends on whether he holds the treasure or not. If the possession of that gold is realized, then the centre of gravity is *in* the individual and no longer in an object on which he depends. To reach such a condition of detachment is the aim of Eastern practices, and it is also the aim of all the teachings of the Church.[216]

---

212 "Tavistock Lectures," § 379.

213 *CW* 9.*ii*, §§ 9, 60.

214 "Psychology of Eastern Meditation," § 945.

215 "A Study in the Process of Individuation," §§ 540-541, and "Concerning Mandala Symbolism," § 638, *CW* 9.*i*; "Tavistock Lectures," §§ 269-71;.

216 "Tavistock Lectures," § 377.

By "impersonal images" Jung means those archetypes—the most fundamental of which is the self—that originate within the psyche and infuse life with meaning by connecting us to a wider horizon. They exist within the individual but sustain a connection to the collective level. Prior to the so-called "fourth stage," we may be aware of these collective symbols, but not as realities that inhere in our own psyches. We know them by projection. Detachment thus consists in recognizing the impersonal images as part of ourselves. This frees us as individuals from dependence on the other. The self as whole symbolizes the resulting self-containment; the full spectrum of symbolic life is available in one's own psychic totality.

The following diagram (5.1) illustrates the change that constitutes the "diamond body." Notice that the world of objects essentially remains unknown in either case, whether one is projecting unconscious contents or not.

Projective Psychology and Divine Transcendence

Jung is the champion of the individual, and his notion of the diamond body reminds us of this fact. What matters most to my argument is what the notion means for the question of a human relation to divine transcendence. To understand what it means, we must notice that projective psychology has become an epistemological stance for Jung. At times he makes extreme statements, such as the following: "The world is our picture. Only childish people imagine that the world is what we think it is. The image of the world is a projection of the world of the self, as the latter is an introjection of the world."[217] Psychological insights into projection—the imputation of internal states onto the other—have come together in this statement with the neo-Kantian subjectivism that I discussed in Chapter 2. At its worst, this results in cutting off the knowing subject from what there is to know.[218]

---

217 Ibid., 120.

218 I also note that the above quotation betrays a hint of the Paracelsian theory that subject and world exist in a symbiotic relationship of microcosmos to cosmos. The world is not only a projection of the psyche, says Jung; the psyche is also an "introjection" of the world.

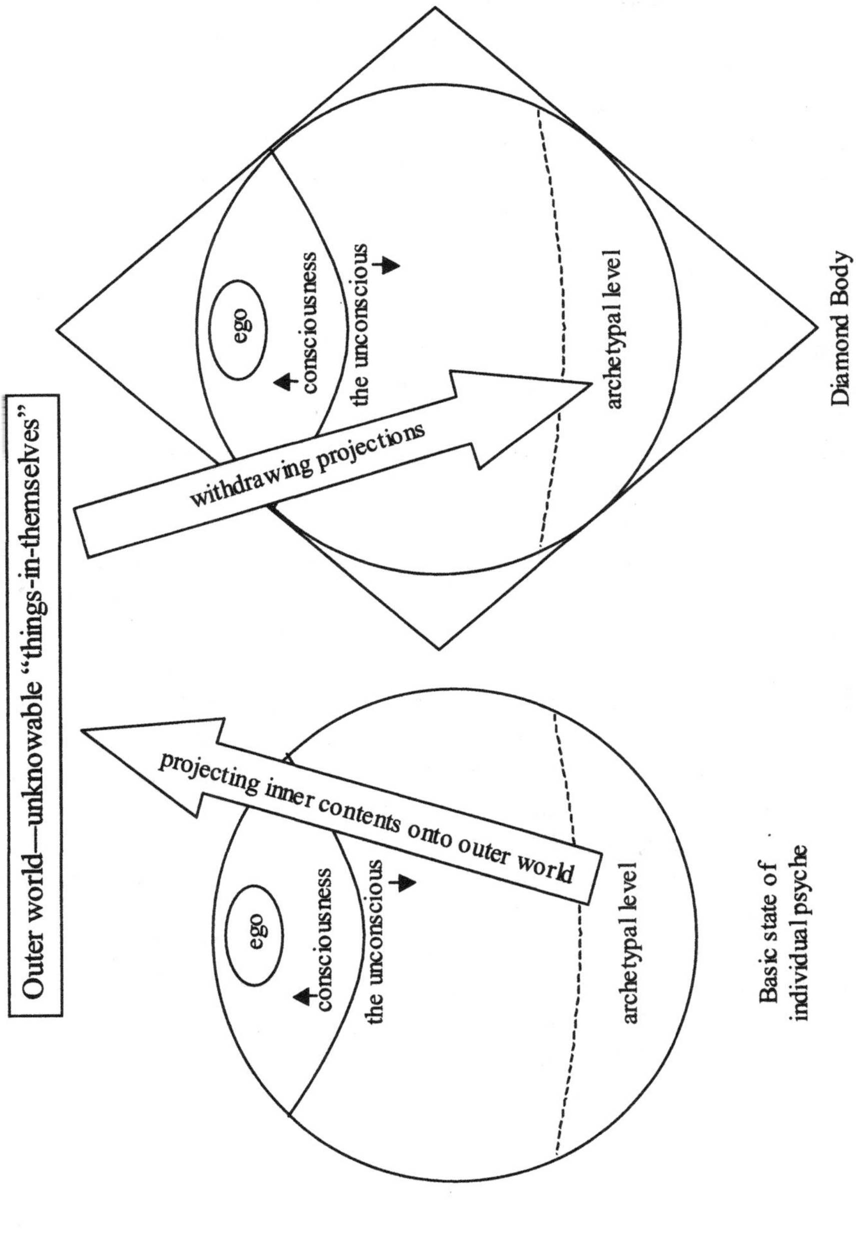
Outer world—unknowable "things-in-themselves"
ego
consciousness
the unconscious
archetypal level
projecting inner contents onto outer world
Basic state of individual psyche
ego
consciousness
the unconscious
archetypal level
withdrawing projections
Diamond Body

Diagram 5.1

Psychology's insights into projective phenomena surely do not give an adequate general account of how we know, and I have already discussed the difficulties with Jung's subjectivism in Chapter 2. Jung never offers a clear remedy to these tendencies in his thought. In accordance with them, he casts contemplative discipline in intrapsychic terms. All is psyche—ego and self, consciousness and the unconscious—and therefore alignment to the self must consist in a descent to the depth of the psyche, not an ascent beyond the psyche towards divine transcendence. The realities involved are wholly immanent, including the reality of god-images, such as the "self" archetype that we project onto a divine being. If we look at Jung from this standpoint, he *does* appear to sit in the same camp as Freud, Nietzsche, Feuerbach, and the rest of the moderns who understand theology as projected anthropology and nothing more.

Jung's usual response to the question of a God beyond projections is not to answer directly but to repeat his belief that we can know only the god-images we find in the psyche, and that we can know nothing of a God beyond these images. Yet, to take an example that illustrates the influence of his subjectivism, his reading of Meister Eckhart makes this mystic an immanentist who came to an enlightened realization of the "relativity" of God as "a function of man." In psychological terms, Eckhart withdrew his projection of the divine image onto a figure external to his own psyche. In so doing, his soul itself became God and was infused with divine energy. The mystic reclaimed the divine image as his own, a psychic content from the depth of the unconscious. Even in this interpretation, however, a divine reality beyond the psyche is not *quite* excluded, since Eckhart felt compelled to distinguish between God and the Godhead and thereby imply a movement of the soul beyond itself.[219]

The following diagram (5.2) illustrates the influence of Jung's subjectivism on his view of contemplative detachment as attainment of the "diamond body." By reclaiming the divine image (the self) as belonging to the psyche, the contemplative becomes infused with the energy previously projected onto the sacred figure of "God."

[219] CW 6, §§ 412-33.

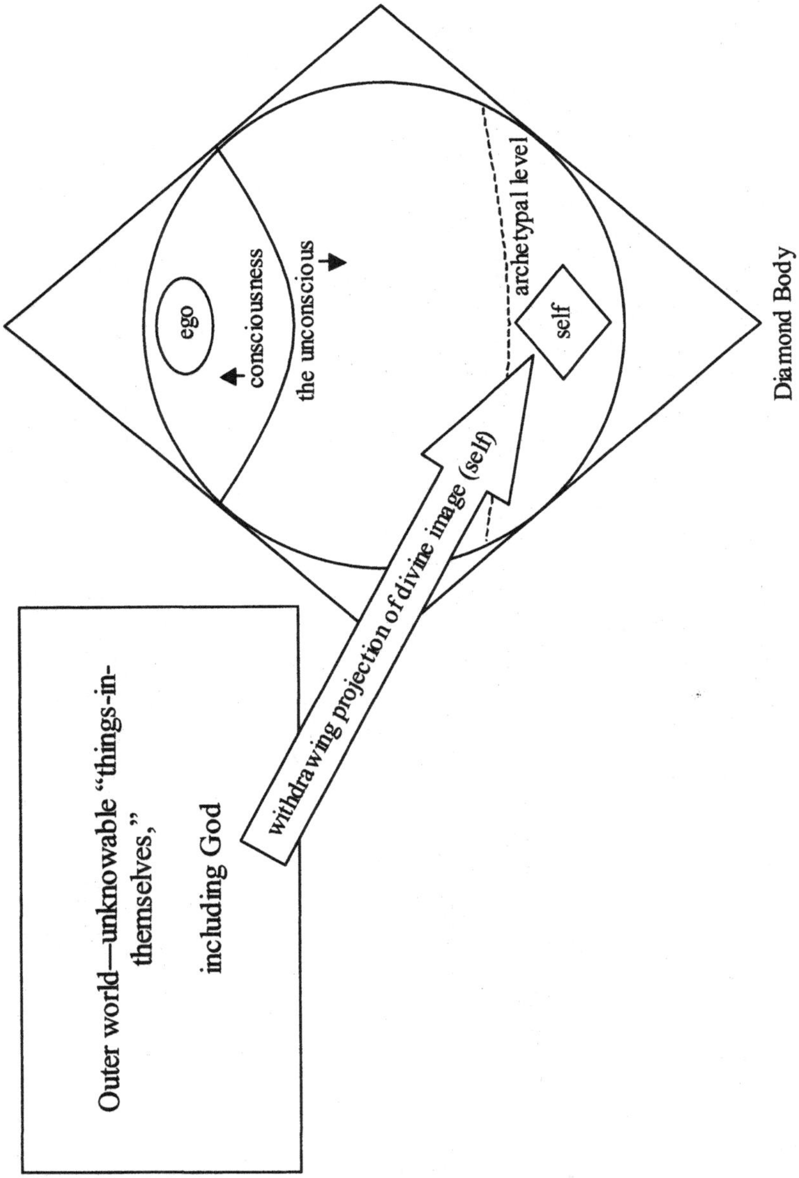
Outer world—unknowable “things-in-themselves,”
including God
withdrawing projection of divine image (self)
ego
consciousness
the unconscious
archetypal level
self
Diamond Body

Diagram 5.2

The Dispute between Jung and Buber

To picture the goal of psychological development as the creation of the individual "diamond body" appears to foreclose the movement of the soul beyond itself towards a transcendent horizon. By finding all that is needed within the vastness of the psyche's depth, the individuated person is following what Jung believed to be an inherent urge in our nature towards independence.[220] Though this is only one aspect of Jung's theory, it is with some justification that Martin Buber in 1952 included Jung in a list of modern thinkers who, according to Buber, have proposed a subjectivism so radical that it completely cuts off the human being from the reality of the transcendent God. These questions about Jung's stance towards the divine still fascinate his readers. In a 2001 article in the *Journal of Analytical Psychology*, Barbara Stephens writes a very engaging account of the disputations between Buber and Jung that followed Buber's accusation; and it is obvious from this article that the controversies over the implications of Jung's thought for theology have never been laid to rest, no matter how many times he denied having made such implications.

Buber's accusation amounts to this: Jung pays attention to religion, but it is not the true religion of the individual's personal relationship to an absolutely transcendent, divine Thou. It is a pseudo-religion in which the devotee merely worships aspects of his or her own psyche. It allows for no real relation to an other-than-I—only a relation to other realities within one's own depths. Jung responded with his usual denial that he had ever made any claims about transcendent being, positive or negative, and argued that he always avoids these questions, which are beyond the competence of psychology. Buber countered that Jung does in fact make a clearly metaphysical assertion when he states that the divine is a component of the human psyche rather than a being that exists independently of the psyche.

---

[220] See the advice Jung gives to an anonymous correspondent in October of 1920. C. G. Jung, *Letters: Volume 1: 1906-1950*, selected and ed. Gerhard Adler, in collaboration with Aniela Jaffé, trans. R. F. C. Hull (Princeton: Princeton University Press, 1973), 78.

This statement, says Buber, makes a claim about the unreality of God. He argues that Jung is a modern "solipsistic mystic."[221]

In his response to Stephens' paper, David Tresan notes the devolution of the disputations into "a kind of reiterative name calling" in which neither disputant appears to have the philosophical grounding adequate to communicate the relation of psychology to the reality of Spirit. He identifies the critical issue for Jung as methodological. From early on, Jung specifically excludes Spirit from his investigations and chooses instead to treat religion as a purely human phenomena open to empirical investigation apart from its relation to a reality beyond the human sphere. Though his empiricism is not the empiricism of the natural sciences, it is radical in its exclusion of what may lie beyond the psyche:

> It was this limited use of mind that Jung espoused in his adoption of a strict, albeit radical, empiricism and an exacting definition of "psychic reality." All reality was perforce psychic experience. This included God experiences and whatever other iconic and schematic data Jung privileged along with their affective, behavioural, and historical concomitants (e.g., archetypes). Because of his empirical standards, which Jung consciously crafted and defended all his life as he did with Buber, what could not qualify for reality was deemed irrelevant. What lay over the horizon of the human mind, nay, the horizon itself, was of no substantive interest to Jung. This included Buber's god. Not-withstanding, because of his careful policing of "reality," Jung paid the price of extrusion. Wittingly or otherwise, the existential seeking quality of pre-Socratic reasoning (***nous***) was split off for Jung into intuition, anima, gnosis, the imaginal, the transcendent function, the religious impulse, and the individuation factor, all of which were enfranchised as reality inhabiting this side of the skyline. In addition, Jung transgressed his own strict empiricism both in periodic trans-ports of pneumatic zeal (see his first book and the last chapter of ***Memories, Dreams, Reflections***) and in postulating non-empirical realities such as the psychoid, ***unus mundus, triton eidos*** (after Plato), and a "neutral language" common to psyche and matter.[222]

Jung seems compelled occasionally to acknowledge a movement in the soul towards what lies beyond itself, but at the same time his self-styled "empiricism" binds him to treat that movement as though it were really a movement towards a beyond *within* the psyche. Tresan astutely notes that this relocation of transcendence to a place within the psyche has the effect of

[221] Barbara D. Stephens, "The Martin Buber-Carl Jung Disputations: Protecting the Sacred in the Battle for the Boundaries of Analytical Psychology," *Journal of Analytical Psychology*, 2001, 46, 455-91; 463-4, 479.

[222] David I. Tresan, "Response to Barbara Stephens's paper in JAP, 46, 3," *Journal of Analytical Psychology*, 2002, 47, 479–502, 496.

foreclosing the "existential seeking quality" that has characterized the search for the divine ground since the pre-Socratics.[223] As Tresan notes, Jung was nevertheless given to episodes of "pneumatic zeal" in spite of his views. We might then reasonably hope to find another interpretation of the symbolic life that does not exclude the movement of seeking for the divine ground.

The Still Point

Jung's notion of the diamond body extends his subjectivism into the symbolic life, implies that symbols for the divine are projected contents of the psyche, and therefore forecloses any movement towards a divine reality beyond the self-contained psyche. But a careful analysis of the symbolic process which he outlines demands a different interpretation, one that does not square well with his epistemological assumptions yet does justice to the realities of symbolic life. My goal in offering this interpretation is to show that symbolic life naturally leads to contemplation of a divine presence that transcends the psyche and its symbolic function. Contemplation of this presence follows recognition of one's own participation in it. This participation is symbolized by a still point of presence that brings the light of consciousness to the flow of symbol formation.

In the elements of symbolic life reiterated at the beginning of this chapter, I find two fundamental movements that pull conscious awareness beyond its normal horizon. The *first movement* begins with the suspension of directed thinking and the consequent activation of the symbol-producing function. The symbol mysteriously arises through the play of dreaming and active imagination, mediates unconscious depth to our awareness, and infuses life with differentiated affect. This process creates an opportunity to recognize that a whole range of psychic activity is at work apart from the ego's normal functioning. Such recognition pulls us beyond our usual horizon of awareness. We know ourselves not simply as the "I" of intentional acts, but as a psyche whose reality extends far beyond the "I." In the *second movement*, we discover a still point from which we apply conscious presence to the flow of symbols activated by the first movement, and do so by neither suppressing nor falling into identity with any of these symbols. The horizon of our awareness then

[223] Other sympathetic readers of Jung have criticized him for this foreclosure of the beyond. See Robert Doran's previously cited essay on "Jung and Catholic Theology," 54.

expands further insofar as we have discovered a new form of conscious presence to ourselves, an engagement in the symbolic flow that is not the *participation mystique* of unalloyed nondirected thinking.

The presence symbolized by the still point solves a problem. Because the first movement activates nondirected thinking, it harkens back to the *participation mystique* of primitive consciousness, in which subject and object are undifferentiated and the conscious attitude is weak. Regression to an undifferentiated state of identity is not the symbolic life; yet a simple *repression* of this primitive style of consciousness would also rule out the symbolic function. For an alignment to psychic depth to take place, we must allow the primitive flow to occur. The ego's directed style of thinking impedes the flow and thus offers no solution. To succeed, we must find a way to allow primitive-like states but keep the differentiation of an intentional subject intact and functioning. Jung seems to think that the diamond body solves this problem, since the individuated person engages in nondirected thinking but refrains from projecting this flow onto the other.

The goal of the diamond body equates the still point with self-containment. Unfortunately, this equation only explains how one gets free from projective identity with the other; it does not explain how one avoids identity with the archetypal layer of one's own psyche. Notice that when comparing the symbolic life to meditative disciplines, Jung often characterizes the change in consciousness that occurs in the practitioner as an experience of the collective unconscious.[224] In his foreword to Suzuki's *Introduction to Zen Buddhism*, he interprets satori as the equivalent to a communication from the unconscious.[225] And in a commentary on *The Tibetan Book of the Great Liberation*, he identifies self-liberation through "One Mind" consciousness as identity with the collective unconscious.[226] In essence, strange as it may sound, he quite clearly implies that the freedom these religious practices offer is a return to *participation mystique*. I feel bound to assume that he would draw a distinction if questioned on this point, but he fails to do so in what I have read.

---

[224] For the Western person, he insists that a strong ego is necessary to resist absorption into the collective unconscious. Yet asserting this need does not in itself adequately differentiate enlightenment from *participation mystique*.

[225] "Foreword to *Introduction to Zen Buddhism*," § 898.

[226] "Psychological Commentary on 'The Tibetan Book of the Great Liberation,'" §§ 783-4.

This view of liberated consciousness drives Jung also to imply that such consciousness involves a complete withdrawal from the outer world, an extreme act of introversion, rather than a newly discovered, enlightened mode of engagement with the world. Such a portrayal does not do justice to the meditative practices that Jung draws on. We would be hard-pressed to find a reliable source that describes satori or similar states in terms consistent with withdrawal into the individual psyche and identity with the collective unconscious. The metaphors typically used to describe enlightened states are not the metaphors of depth, but of ascent and light, not of the unconscious, but of consciousness. *The Golden Flower*, for instance, speaks of the "circulation of the light"—the light, that is, of attentive consciousness.

Perhaps Jung would have denied these misrepresentations if pressed. I am not being entirely fair, to be sure, but I must push the implication of what he writes to its extreme in order to illustrate a problem. The problem originates in his use of the penultimate symbol of depth and wholeness—the self—to describe the discovery of the still point. Wholeness and depth symbolism simply do not fit the phenomenon of the still point. According to Jung, when the self symbolizes undifferentiated wholeness, it is pointing to a source of creative order that lies in the depths awaiting activation: "The beginning, in which everything is still one, and which therefore appears as the highest god, lies at the bottom of the sea in the darkness of the unconscious."[227] Such symbols are numinous, certainly, but I propose that the still point is not this wholeness in the depth. Neither is it the "whole" as the collective unconscious. Neither is it the diamond body as a self-contained psyche. Rather, it is the differentiation of a mode of *conscious presence to* the symbols that arise from the depth, including the various symbols of undifferentiated wholeness. The still point is not the depth or the whole; it is conscious presence to the depth and the whole.

Jung does not generally speak of presence at the still point in this way. He prefers the symbolism of depth and descent into the psyche over the symbolism of ascent and the light of conscious presence. Yet according to my analysis, his preference misleads him. The still point's conscious presence is *not*:

- the participation mystique of pure nondirected thinking;
- a state of identity with the collective unconscious;

[227] *The Golden Flower*, 101.

- the withdrawing of projections that in Jung's view creates a diamond body; or
- the directed thinking of the intentional ego.

And this presence *is* a mode of being:

- consciously aware (a "presence") in symbolic life that is distinct from any of the modes just listed;
- gained through some form of spiritual discipline, such as meditation or practice of the symbolic life;
- able to exist simultaneously with the flow of nondirected thinking;
- able to facilitate symbol formation;
- productive of consciousness to the symbolic function, where our usual directed style of thinking would interfere; and
- making possible differentiated symbol formation in that (a) without consciousness the symbolic flow is technically mere *participation mystique*; (b) directed thinking cannot bring conscious presence to the symbolic flow adequately, since it interferes with nondirected thinking; (c) another way of bringing consciousness to the symbolic function is therefore necessary; and (d) the presence of the still point fulfills this need.

Understanding the symbolic function in Jung's thought requires us to acknowledge both a descent and an ascent—first, a descent into the depth of the psyche, facilitated by nondirected thinking and, second, an ascent towards a still point of presence. On account of the descent, symbols arise which communicate unconscious affect. On account of the ascent, these symbols exist as symbols rather than as states of primitive identity with the unconscious. Since directed thinking quells the symbolic function, a new differentiation of consciousness is required, one that coexists with the symbolic flow but is clearly distinct from that flow. I believe that the presence symbolized in *The Golden Flower* as a still point—a consciousness without contents that nonetheless allows all contents to exist—is this new differentiation. The act of exercising its presence achieves two conditions for the possibility of symbolic life: distinction from *participation mystique* and conscious nearness to the symbols formed at the level of *participation mystique*. Presence is differentiated from—therefore distinct from—yet at the same moment intimately present with the symbolic level. That is to say, it *transcends* the symbolic level.

Diagram 5.3 shows the movements I am describing. Notice that the symbol occurs only between the still point of presence and the depth of the unconscious, and only when presence reaches down in openness to those dreams and fantasies that are arising from the depth. The symbol is differentiated from both the still point and the depth but would not exist without their concurrence. Further, the creation of a symbol requires an intentional human subject, the "individual," who is also existing between the still point and the depth and in whom the differentiation of presence occurs as a result of the ascent required to appropriate the descent. The subject does not exist in undifferentiated identity with either the still point or the depth but participates in the reality of both. In my view, which is a development of Jung's thought, the differentiation of these four—still point, depth, subject, and symbol—is what constitutes the symbolic function in its full sense. From a formal standpoint, this function requires the existence of each of the four and the five noted relations between them. I have designated the relations in the diagram as (1) the "downward" openness of presence to depth; (2) what arises from depth to presence; (3) the subject's ascent to the still point; (4) the subject's descent into depth; and (5) the subject's appropriation of the symbol.

The Beyond

Jung himself notes that mystics from West and East have described a highly dramatic participation in divine light that uses the same language of illumination which characterizes ascent to the still point:

> The phenomenon itself, that is, the vision of light, is an experience common to many mystics, and one that is undoubtedly of the greatest significance, because in all times and places it appears as the unconditional thing, which unites in itself the greatest energy and the profoundest meaning. Hildegarde of Bingen, an outstanding personality quite apart from her mysticism, expresses herself about her central vision in a similar way. "Since my childhood," she says, "I have always seen a light in my soul, but not with the outer eyes, nor through the thoughts of my heart; neither do the five outer senses take part in this vision....The light I perceive is not of a local kind, but is much brighter than the cloud which bears the sun. I cannot distinguish height, breadth, or length in it.... What I see or learn in such a vision stays long in my memory. I see, hear, and know in the same moment.... I cannot recognize any sort of form in this light, although I sometimes see in it another light that is known to me as the living light....While I am enjoying the spectacle of this light, all sadness and sorrow vanish from my memory...."[228]

[228] Ibid., 106 (reference to quote from Hildegarde not given).

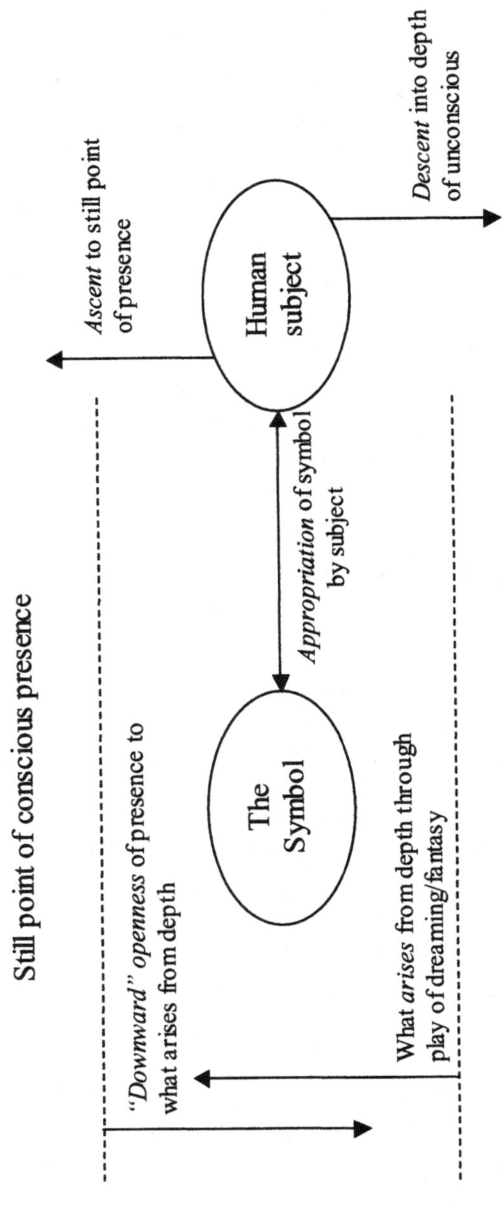
Still point of conscious presence
"Downward" openness of presence to what arises from depth
The Symbol
Appropriation of symbol by subject
Human subject
Ascent to still point of presence
What arises from depth through play of dreaming/fantasy
Descent into depth of unconscious
Depth of unconscious psyche

Diagram 5.3

When we understand the still point properly, it becomes clear that however we see its relation to divine presence, we cannot explain it as a "psychic content"—an inner god-image in the psyche—projected onto God. In depth psychologies, a psychic content consists in a something—a complex, an image, etc.—whose existence we can objectify as a discrete reality in the psyche. Yet if we try to identify our conscious presence at the still point as such a content, we will hopefully recognize that *only through our acts of conscious presence* do we identify "contents" of the psyche. The reality of presence makes these identifications possible. And while we can objectify contents without participating in them, we cannot objectify presence without participating in it. We then come face-to-face with the fact that we cannot explain away as projection the mystic's understanding of presence as a participation in divine light. The understanding may be false, but it does not constitute a projection in the usual sense of that term.

I believe that a movement of faith naturally begins to take place at this juncture in those whose spiritual practice has culminated in the recognition of the still point's reality. The still point provides an analogy by which faith can understand how God is present to consciousness—differentiated from us, yet near to our hearts. In other words, it provides us with a more adequate notion of transcendence. Although the bulk of modern thought would rally against a movement of faith that understands presence at the still point as a participation in divine presence, of created light in uncreated light, the foreclosure of such a movement is not universal. To show that it is not universal, I will briefly summarize the way in which philosopher Eric Voegelin uses the symbol "presence" to indicate the participation of human consciousness in divine light. The relevance of Voegelin's work to the study of mythology is well-known and made explicit by the philosopher himself, as is his analysis of various theological symbols; but so far as I know he does not venture into the arena of psychotherapy and symbols as mediators of affective depth. He does, however, analyze extensively the symbol of the "Beyond" of divine presence and its revelatory ordering of the soul, and this analysis illuminates the contemplative movement from the still point towards the divine presence in which it participates.

Michael Morrissey distinguishes the two fundamental transcendent symbols in Voegelin's late work:

> "Beginning" refers to the primary experience of the cosmos which historically found expression in creation myths, while "beyond" alludes to the revelatory awakening of

> divine presence in the soul in mystic experience, to the transcendent realm that gives history and the soul an eschatological direction.[229]

To each of these primary symbols belongs a category of revelation.

> Divine reality is being revealed to man in two fundamental modes of experience: in the experience of divine creativity in the cosmos; and in the experience of divine ordering presence in the soul.
>
> The two modes are always structures in man's consciousness of divine reality, but they are not always conscious in the form of reflected knowledge....[230]

The second of these modes correlates to the still point in symbolic life. The Beyond makes itself present in the soul's movements, and this "requires the revelatory language of consciousness. This is the language of seeking, searching, and questioning, of ignorance and knowledge concerning the divine ground, of futility, absurdity, anxiety, and alienation of existence, of being turned around, of return, illumination, and rebirth."[231]

Further, it requires a language of presence. The reality of the Beyond experienced in the contemplative movement of consciousness towards its ground is not like the reality of things, according to Voegelin, who instead describes it as a presence, the "Parousia of the Beyond" that brings to the temporal world the nontemporal dimension of an "indelible present."[232] The human questioner's meditative acts are the site of these influxes of Parousia, which reveal the participatory nature of consciousness. Instead of understanding consciousness as a self-contained psyche standing in opposition to objects in the world, Voegelin understands consciousness as a participation in the divine ground of existence. The "I" does not constitute either consciousness or the realities of which we are conscious. Rather, we are seeking participants in an intelligible reality that includes both intentional subjects and the world of objects. In Glenn Hughes' words,

---

[229] Michael Morrissey, *Consciousness and Transcendence: The Theology of Eric Voegelin* (Notre Dame: University of Notre Dame Press, 1994), 283.

[230] Eric Voegelin, "The Beginning and the Beyond: A Meditation on Truth," in *What is History? And Other Late Unpublished Writings*, volume 28 in *The Collected Works of Eric Voegelin*, ed. Thomas A. Hollweck and Paul Caringella (Baton Rouge: Louisiana State University Press, 1990), 173.

[231] Eric Voegelin, *Order and History, v. 4, The Ecumenic Age* (Baton Rouge: LSU Press, 1974), 17-18.

[232] Eric Voegelin, *Order and History, v. 5, In Search of Order*, ed. Ellis Sandoz (Columbia: University of Missouri Press, 2000), 30.

> The data that forms the "material" for the insight that the finite cosmos has as its ground a reality that is other than finite being is the "movement of the soul," as Voegelin puts it, that discovers its own nature both to presuppose and to be co-constituted by a spiritual reality unrestricted by finite limitations. Unless consciousness finds itself engaged in the questioning tension that so desires to identify the true ground of reality that it finds all the splendors of the cosmos still not enough to explain and satisfy its own restless capacity to think and feel *beyond* those splendors, then there can be no occasion for an epiphany of transcendence. When such a movement does occur, what has happened, in Voegelin's terms, is that the tension of consciousness toward a reality beyond all cosmic contents has become transparent for its own nature as "spiritual," i.e., as related by participation to a ground that is incommensurate with limitation. Of course such a ground is known only in the interiority of meditation and reflection, and so it is nothing in the world that can be pointed to.[233]

According to this account, the questioner is the "site" of the Beyond revealing itself in the soul's movement towards that same Beyond. The Beyond lies at both ends of the quest—as mover and as that towards which one moves. It is therefore a truly *transpersonal* presence operative in the consciousness of the person. The symbolic life can lead naturally to this revelation of the divine ground. If the still point of presence becomes differentiated, this differentiation may ignite in the human subject a quest for a presence that like the still point is both distinct and near, yet unlike the still point is *absolutely* "incommensurate with limitation"—infinitely, not finitely, transcendent. Faith can then understand this divine Parousia as the source and analogue of finite presence to oneself. After all, the still point symbolizes the conscious presence that lies at the beginning of the symbolic life as a movement that opens itself to the depth, and at the end of the symbolic life as the presence to which one returns in recognition of the conscious differentiation that made it possible to know the symbol.

We can represent the dynamics I am suggesting in the following diagram (5.4). Here we see (1) a "bottom-up" movement of the subject reaching out to the still point that makes symbolic life possible and finding that the still point engenders wonder about the transcendent origins of its own formative reality; and (2) a "top-down" movement in which the reality of divine transcendence as a formative presence in consciousness reveals itself through the formative presence of the still point.

---

233 Glenn Hughes, *Mystery and Myth in the Philosophy of Eric Voegelin* (Columbia: University of Missouri Press, 1993), 52-4.

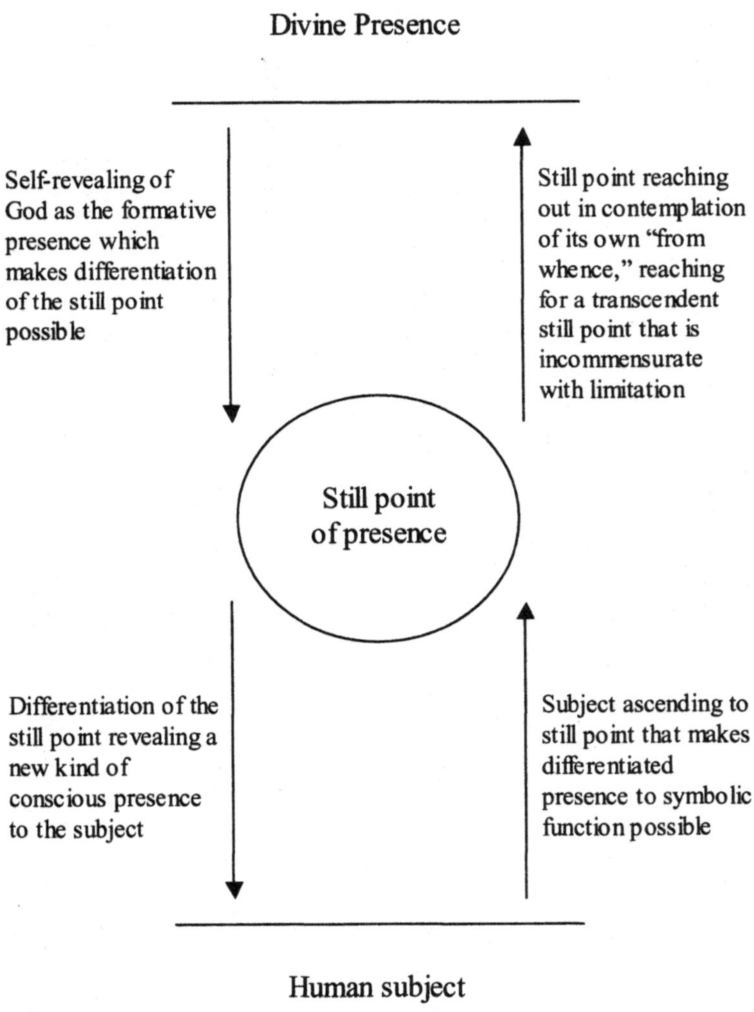
Divine Presence
Self-revealing of God as the formative presence which makes differentiation of the still point possible
Still point reaching out in contemplation of its own "from whence," reaching for a transcendent still point that is incommensurate with limitation
Still point of presence
Differentiation of the still point revealing a new kind of conscious presence to the subject
Subject ascending to still point that makes differentiated presence to symbolic function possible
Human subject

Diagram 5.4

If finding in the symbolic life an occasion for divine presence to reveal itself strikes the modern reader as exceedingly strange, this impression may stem from the assumption that human reality is confined either to the physical level or—at most, as for Jung—to the psychological level. In Voegelin's analysis, human existence is fundamentally constituted by spiritual realities, by irreducible conscious acts that open us to the divine ground. He believes that two main symbolisms in the West have served to articulate the formative divine presence in consciousness: from Plato and Aristotle the symbol *nous*, often translated "intellect," and from biblical tradition the symbol *pneuma* (or *ruach* in the Hebrew), often translated "Spirit." Though Voegelin does not consider these symbols identical, they both "indicate the site where transcendent divine and human consciousness enjoy the intimacy of participation."[234]

We learned in chapter 2 that Jung clung from early on to his belief that an immaterial reality, the soul or psyche, is operative in human existence. As far back as the Zofingia lectures of his student days, he began building his notion of "the reality of the psyche." I have concluded that in "the symbolic life" an immaterial reality does in fact operate. But this reality is one of presence that leads beyond the notion of the psyche as a self-contained, immaterial entity. Presence challenges the notion that the psyche exists in such a way that we can unreservedly describe it in this language. Instead, I have proposed that the spiritual characteristics of presence bring us to understand the psyche and its symbolic function as a reality oriented beyond itself, towards the spiritual reality of divine presence.

Contemporary Psychoanalysis and the Still Point

Having found an interpretation of Jung's symbolic life that does not foreclose the soul's contemplation of divine transcendence, I now turn to several contemporary psychoanalytic authors whose understanding of symbol formation adds to what we have gained from Jung. I will ask whether their work also leads us to recognize the spiritual reality of presence and the contemplative ascent to divine presence. First, I will review a recent article by Barbara Stephens that shows the emergence of "Jungian" themes in contemporary psychoanalysis. Second, I will examine the theory of symbol

[234] Ibid., 55.

formation that contemporary psychoanalyst Thomas Ogden presents in his essay on "Potential Space." Third, I will show that several authors commonly seen as Ogden's peers have written about the spiritual presence involved in symbolic formation.

Stephens writes on the emergence of so-called "Jungian" themes in post-Freudian thought. Her provocatively entitled article, "The Return of the Prodigal," traces "a number of Jungian concepts which sit on the self-proclaimed 'cutting edge' of psychoanalytic theory."[235] She begins by pointing to recent questions whether Freud and Jung diverge so fundamentally in their philosophical allegiances as most have thought. Some argue that not only Jung, but Freud as well, structures his psychology along mythological lines. Having failed to reduce the "drives" to clear biological causes, Freud posited them as *a priori* theoretical entities whose existence we cannot demonstrate by natural scientific methods. They function in Freud much as archetypes function in Jung. In light of such reevaluations of basic psychoanalytic assumptions, many contemporary psychoanalysts have abandoned the hard science aspirations of their tradition. These thinkers generally find themselves grouped together as "intersubjectivists" and include Theodore Jacobs, Owen Renik, James Grotstein, Thomas Ogden, and others.

All share a strong emphasis on the primacy of the intersubjective reality that exists in the consulting room. That is, they emphasize the primacy for psychoanalytic theory of two persons engaging in a particular type of conversation that encourages a meditative, nondirected style of consciousness.[236] We cannot divorce the insights gained by attending to such conversations from their intersubjective context. The contemporary psychoanalyst does not pretend to act as a neutral party observing the data of patient associations. Rather, the data originate from the intersubjective reality of the conversation, and even the analyst's mental experience is not simply his or her own. It too belongs to the patient/analyst dyad.[237] Thus counter-transferences are not just unconscious interference; they provide important clues to the movement of the therapy. To Stephens this primacy of *psychology*

---

[235] Barbara Stephens, "The Return of the Prodigal: The Emergence of Jungian Themes in Post-Freudian Thought," *Journal of Analytical Psychology*, 44 (1999); 197-220, 198.

[236] That is, a style akin to what Jung proposes for symbolic life. Whereas Jung generally recommended its use outside the consulting room in the work of active imagination, these thinkers recommend it as a form of "reverie" useful for cultivating symbol formation within the analytic relationship.

[237] Stephens, 202.

over biology sounds much like Jung's commitment to the psyche's irreducible reality.[238]

To engage in analysis requires a discipline that these authors often describe in religious language. One must open oneself to whatever arises, learn to be content with a state of not knowing, and, in Wilfred Bion's words, empty oneself of memory and desire. Such meditative virtues provide the conditions that allow the symbolic development of the therapy to take place. With Jung, the intersubjectivists trust that given the proper conditions, the symbolic process will lead to the needed therapeutic benefit.[239] In other words, they implicitly trust in the psyche's purposiveness. This trust leads some of them to use mystical language for the unknown source of psychic order and growth, such as "true self," "bipolar self," "O," or "Subject" with a capital S.[240]

Ogden on Potential Space

Of the "cutting edge" psychoanalytic theorists, Thomas Ogden has written perhaps the most significant essay on symbol formation. "Potential Space" outlines his understanding of Donald Winnicott's concept of the same name. In this essay, we find many of the essential elements that characterize the contemporary movement that Stephens writes about. Potential space for Winnicott indicates "an intermediate area of experiencing that lies between fantasy and reality. Specific forms of potential space include the play space, the area of the transitional object and phenomena, the analytic space, the area of cultural experience, and the area of creativity." Since Winnicott expresses his concept in a difficult series of images and metaphors, Ogden sums up its meaning for his reader and shows that the capacity to generate potential space in turn generates the capacity to symbolize and ultimately to become a subject.[241]

Ogden begins with a definition of "subjectivity":

> By subjectivity, I am referring to the capacity for degrees of self-awareness ranging from intentional self-reflection (a very late achievement) to the most subtle, unobtrusive sense of "I-ness" by which experience is subtly endowed with the quality

[238] Ibid., 200-1.

[239] Ibid., 207-10.

[240] Ibid., 209, 205.

[241] Thomas Ogden, "Potential Space," in *The Matrix of the Mind: Object Relations and the Psychoanalytic Dialogue* (Northvale, NJ: Jason Aronson, 1993), 203.

> that one is thinking one's thoughts and feeling one's feelings as opposed to living in a state of reflexive reactivity. Subjectivity is related to, but not the same as, consciousness. The experience of consciousness (and unconsciousness) follows from the achievement of subjectivity. Subjectivity, as will be discussed, is a reflection of the differentiation of symbol, symbolized, and interpreting subject.[242]

For a human being to start on the way to achieving subjectivity, certain developmental successes must occur in early life, beginning with mother and infant. According to Winnicott, these two exist at first interdependently as a "mother-infant" unity. The beginnings of an infant's subjectivity depend on a transition from this primal unity to what Ogden calls the dialectical relation between an I and an other-than-I. Optimally, the transition begins to take place when feelings of separateness first occur in the infant. When the infant recognizes the mother as an other-than-I, then not only the I becomes constituted, but the other (the mother) does so as well. Acts of conscious differentiation arise in the mother-infant unity and constitute the two's eventual separation.

Assuming that a "good-enough" fit exists between mother and infant, their unity preserves itself for a developmentally appropriate length of time by excluding disturbing intimations of separateness. In Winnicott's view, these intimations generally begin somewhere between four to twelve months in age. When they do begin, the capacity for potential space becomes critical, for a healthy transition to twoness requires such space. He uses the word "potential" because the twoness at this stage is not actual and absolute. Rather, the space "is filled with the state of mind that embodies the never-challenged paradox: The infant and mother are one, and the infant and mother are two."[243] On the way to differentiating I and other-than-I, the infant finds the capacity to "be alone in the presence of the mother." The "transitional object" symbolically embodies this paradoxical oneness/twoness and mediates a sense of mother's presence to the infant, even when she is physically absent.

The generation of potential space should continue in the next developmental stage, where a further differentiation to threeness takes place: "...the symbol (a thought), the symbolized (that which is being thought about), and the interpreting subject (the thinker generating his own thoughts and interpreting his own symbols)." The growth of subjectivity occurs when symbol, symbolized, and subject exist in relation to each other. Within this triad, human beings engage in the meaning-making that distinguishes them

---

[242] Ibid., 208-9.

[243] Ibid., 212.

from purely reflexive beings.[244] If any of the three relations (subject/symbol, symbol/symbolized, subject/symbolized) "dedifferentiates," then subjectivity ceases to exist. Ogden lays the groundwork (via Winnicott) to define subjectivity as the capacity to maintain the dialectics of I and other-than-I through symbol-creating activity:

> The establishment of the distinction between the symbol and the symbolized is inseparable from the establishment of subjectivity: the two achievements are two facets of the same developmental event. Paraphrasing Winnicott, one could say that potential space lies between the symbol and the symbolized. To distinguish symbol from symbolized is to distinguish one's thought from that which one is thinking about, one's feeling from that which one is responding to. For symbol to stand independently of symbolized, there must be a subject engaged in the process of interpreting perceptions. One might ask what is new in this supposed developmental advance, because logically there has always been a person interpreting his experience. That is, of course, so from an outside observer's point of view, but it has not been so from the subject's point of view. In fact, a subject did not exist when symbol and symbolized were undifferentiable.[245]

From this abstract presentation comes a theory of psychopathological malformations in human beings. If fantasy subsumes the capacity to symbolize, the world becomes two-dimensional. No symbolic meanings convey experience to the subject. Only a concretistic experience takes place: "The hallucination does not sound like a voice, it *is* a voice. One's husband does not simply behave coldly, he *is* ice. One does not feel like one's father, one's father *is* in one's blood and must be bled out in order for one to be free of him."[246] We find much the same notion in Jung's term "unconscious identity." Secondly, if on account of trauma or some other cause, the play of imaginative meanings produces terrifying anxiety, the individual stops the play and forecloses the subjective dialectic. Life becomes flat, bereft of affect. Finally, symbol and symbolized can dissociate from one another when the subject fears a traumatic set of meanings or, in more extreme cases, ceases attributing meaning to experience at all and leaves only raw perception and the total absence of subjectivity.[247]

Though he (like Jung) does not explicitly differentiate presence as a conscious reality distinct from either subjectivity or reflexive reactivity, Ogden explains that in order for the triad of symbol-symbolized-subject to function

---

[244] Ibid., 213.

[245] Ibid., 224-5.

[246] Ibid., 216.

[247] Ibid., 216-224.

and make subjectivity possible, the developing child must have felt the real presence of the mother. Does this need cease when the child achieves healthy subjectivity? Other contemporary authors use religious language to indicate a presence that continues to operate in adults and to make the imaginative play of symbol formation possible. For example, John McDargh draws on Winnicott to argue that we must understand transitional objects and play in order to understand object representations of God. Transitional objects mediate between the inner world of feelings and the outer world of things. This mediation enables the child to feel the parent's presence and enjoy the safe holding environment in which play can take place. "Play for Winnicott, as it was for Erikson, is the serious work of childhood. It involves trying on roles and identities, experimenting with a range of possible emotions, manipulating the external world for the satisfaction of an inner vision. More generally, it means relaxing one's need to respond and react so as to act out of a spontaneous, creative core of self."[248]

Transitional objects carry the parent's presence into contexts where the parent cannot come, or where the child has begun to separate and needs to invest an intermediate object as a symbol of the parent's continuing presence. When a person puts faith in God, McDargh argues, then God functions for that person as a presence in the company of which the "true self" manifests itself in creative play: "for some persons God functions as that all accepting Other who, like the analyst and the good-enough mother, is the guarantor and preserver of that background of safety which makes possible play."[249] He argues that object relations theorist W.R.D. Fairbairn "allows what Freud would never have considered, that understood rightly religion and psychoanalysis aim for the same results, and under some circumstances religion may be the more effective of the two."[250] This aim is to come into a saving relationship with the other—for religion, with the divine Other, and for psychoanalysis, with the personal presence of the therapist. The sufferer hopes to find freedom from bondage to oppressive object relationships and schizoid isolation.

Psychoanalyst Michael Eigen also searches for a way to speak of the mysterious presence that continues even in adult life to operate as a condition for play. In his seminal article, "The Area of Faith in Winnicott, Lacan and

---

[248] John McDargh, *Psychoanalytic Object Relations Theory and the Study of Religion: On Faith and the Imaging of God* (Lanham, MD: University Press, 1983), 226-7.

[249] Ibid., 229.

[250] Ibid., 207. "Objects" in the psychoanalytic context refers to our most fundamental interpersonal attachments with others.

Bion," he begins by arguing that Winnicott's insight into transitional experiencing shows the primacy of the infant's nonreflective faith that there is space in the world for his or her spontaneous, creative play. Later in the article, he explicates the role of faith in Bion's picture of the analytic relationship, a relationship which ideally provides the "wholling" presence in which the patient and analyst are able to exercise faith by attending truthfully to spontaneously arising thoughts, feelings, and symbolic phenomena. Bion calls the reality to which the two attend "O"— his peculiar symbol for the "ultimate reality" or "God" that reveals itself in the analytic hour.

Bion insisted that the analyst use discipline and free the mind from memory and desire. Eigen lucidly points out that this insistence essentially calls for faith rather than mastery, for truthful acknowledgment of what *is* rather than manipulation aimed at achieving control. Truth in Bion means telling the truth about the feelings, sensations, and thoughts that occur to the two persons engaged in the analytic relationship. Eigen insists that maintaining a courageous openness to these realities makes very great demands on both individuals:

> Attention to the emotional truth of situations must have a certain independence of pleasure-pain considerations. One cannot "regulate" the movement of truth. Rather, one seeks to modulate oneself in relation to requirements that truth discloses. The containing function, at bottom, seeks to influence the movement of O in ego desirable directions, in fathomable and manipulable terms. It aims to cut one's ultimate reality to ego size. Ordinary good adaptations may make life manageable, but may diminish chances for profound psychic transformation. The natural attitude, however supportive and useful, is not the analytic attitude and can interfere with the most far-reaching kinds of therapeutic encounters. To try to control where truth will lead is to put oneself above truth, and so, in part, shut out the potentially reorienting effects of the latter. To maximize the possibility of contact with what is most important for becoming at one with oneself, the subject must relate to truth with faith.[251]

Notice that he does not oppose faith to fact. He defines faith as a non-defensive movement of the soul towards the truth of what one is experiencing. For Bion, faith in truth does not primarily defend one against anxiety, but functions as "an intrinsic principle of emotional growth."[252] Although Eigen does not conflate Bion with Winnicott (or Lacan), he notes the important

[251] Michael Eigen, "The Area of Faith in Winnicott, Lacan and Bion," in *Relational Psychoanalysis: The Emergence of a Tradition*, ed. Stephen Mitchell and Lewis Aron (Hillsdale, NJ: The Analytic Press, 1999), 22.

[252] Ibid., 32.

connections, because the invitation to exercise faith in truth (Bion) comes when *play* (Winnicott) presents us with unconscious material to tell the truth about.

Though philosophical dialectic differs greatly from psychotherapeutic conversation, I would like to recall Lawrence's identification of something akin to "faith in truth," the natural impulse towards truth-seeking that he sees as essential to authentic personhood. Remember that he sees dialectic as midwife to the "self-transcending, transpersonal impulse at the core of the truth intention." I believe that Eigen (as well as Bion) has discovered a similar truth intention that operates in psychotherapeutic conversation. It includes the conversants in a horizon wider than the merely personal. For both Lawrence and Eigen, authentic personhood—"subjectivity"—depends on faithful exercise of a self-transcending desire for truth. In the consulting room, this desire demands that the conversants let go of the dishonest structures by which they attempt to protect themselves from the emotional realities that faith in truth is revealing.

In the book's conclusion, I will relate the transcendent principle of "faith in truth" to the differentiation of the still point necessary for symbolic life. In the meantime, the following diagram (5.5) shows the relations between "play" or "reverie" (forms of nondirected thinking), faith in truth, and parental presence. Without the ascent towards parental presence, exercising faith in truth towards the unconscious products of play would not occur. This requirement presumably stems from the need to feel a loving presence when facing what arises from the unknown depth.

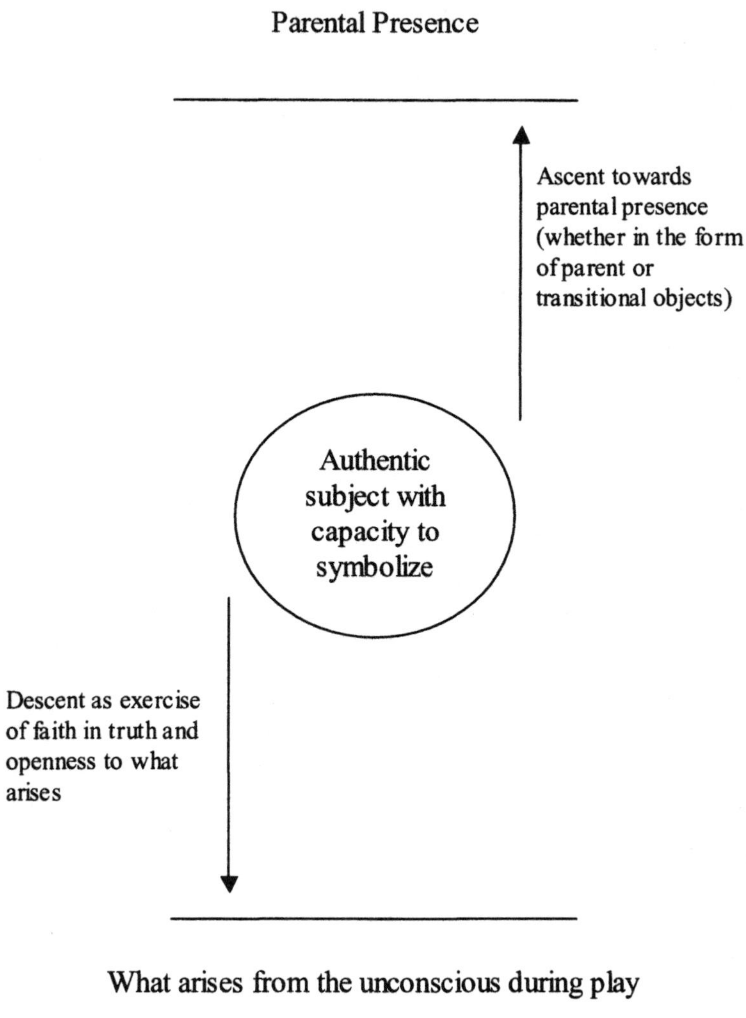
Parental Presence
Ascent towards parental presence (whether in the form of parent or transitional objects)
Authentic subject with capacity to symbolize
Descent as exercise of faith in truth and openness to what arises
What arises from the unconscious during play

Diagram 5.5

• CHAPTER SIX •

Conclusion

My reader will remember from Chapter 1 that Rieff declared modern therapeutic man free from any "suspicions of divinity." Ironically, this turn of phrase perfectly characterizes those contemporary psychoanalysts I have discussed. They have a definite but under-developed intimation of a transcendent presence at work in the symbolic process.[253] For instance, Eigen's insight into Bion's "O" and "faith in truth" clearly plays an integral role in his work and amounts to much more than a useful fiction offered as a simulation of true faith.[254] For these "psychoanalytic mystics," [255] a human being exists in a manner fundamentally open to a beyond that they have only begun to differentiate in their written works. The sense of mystery in their writings comes through strongly, but how far it takes them towards contemplation of what Voegelin calls the divine ground remains unsure. They have teased out the implications of finite presences for subjectivity and intersubjectivity, yet understandably seldom comment on the movement of faith that turns from the finite to the infinite.

To recognize the still point as a created participation in uncreated presence, we must ask what lies beyond the finite horizon; and neither Jung nor the psychoanalytic mystics generally allow this question into the conversation. Yet both describe the play of non-directed thinking in similar terms; both recognize the necessity of practicing meditative discipline to

[253] Rieff, 61.

[254] Other relevant examples include James Grotstein's "numinous Subject" and "transcendent position" and Ogden's hypothesis that there exists an intersubjective subject–the "analytic third." James Grotstein, "The numinous and immanent nature of the psychoanalytic Subject," *Journal of Analytical Psychology* 43 (1998): 41-68; Thomas Ogden, "The Analytic Third: Working with Intersubjective Clinical Facts," in *Relational Psychoanalysis: The Emergence of a Tradition.*

[255] Michael Eigen's term.

facilitate the symbolic function; and in both I find that these matters of practice lead into theological questions of the Beyond, just as they always have led for contemplatives West and East. But we must allow the horizon of permissible questions to expand with the natural movement of seeking. If the question of a presence "incommensurate with limitation" arises—a presence transcending that of mother, transitional object, analyst, or still point—we must allow this question into the conversation. Not to do so would extinguish the seeking quality of our wondering.

The overwhelmingly strong precedent of modernity tells us to stop the movement of seeking from venturing beyond the finite horizon. One reason for this precedent, we must admit, originates in depth psychology itself. Though we read in Chapter 2 about its origins in French psychopathology, its heritage also includes the modern "hermeneuts of suspicion": Feuerbach, Nietzsche, and Freud, who explain divinity as projected anthropology. In Chapter 1 we saw that Rieff's now rather old book retains the spirit of this suspicion, for even his nostalgia for "sacred order" and the "vertical in authority" is tinged with modernity's secret knowledge that sacred order all along amounted only to a power play for the sake of social harmony. Until very recently, and for the most part even now, this suspicion remained unquestioned in Freudian circles; and very likely new research in object relations, attachment theory, and related disciplines will further increase our understanding of the anthropological components in our object representations of God.

Like any depth psychologist, Jung analyzes projections; and this analysis along with his refusal to speak of things outside the psyche left him defenseless against Buber, who argued that he had excluded the transcendent God. My research has found no final resolution to Jung's philosophical subjectivism. Yet I think we still have much to gain from his phenomenology of the symbolic function. He based this work on the depth psychological insights whose history Ellenberger chronicles. Once he understood the psyche to include an unconscious pole that speaks in mythopoetic language, he went on quite naturally to find the conditions that facilitate symbol formation. He then faced the difficulty, however, of how to revive the symbolic depth of the psyche without sacrificing the differentiation of subject and object that marks progress over the primitive state of *participation mystique*.

No wonder Jung and Buber reached such an impasse in their disputations. Interpreting religious symbols as products of the psyche's mythopoetic function does not add up to an authentic relation with a divine Thou—at least not on the face of it. Yet Tresan notes that later in life Jung had experiences of "pneumatic zeal" that drew him towards a transcendent Spirit that defied his empirical rule of excluding what is not psyche. My strategy has been to show that quite apart from his philosophical subjectivism, the practices that he recommends for living the symbolic life allow for and even lead to a contemplative turn towards Spirit.

When symbols arise from the depth of the psyche, we feel an invitation to open ourselves to their deep affective resonance; at the same time, we feel an invitation to recognize the still point to which we have ascended in order to exercise conscious presence to the symbols that have arisen. This presence of the still point constitutes a further differentiation of consciousness beyond directed thinking *or* nondirected thinking—one in which we relate to symbolic experience with an intimate nearness, attention, imaginative elaboration, and emotional development, and yet do not fall into identity with the unconscious. Our presence functions unbounded by complexes and other "contents" of the psyche. Yet it is the very reality that makes conscious intimacy with these contents possible.

Openness to the symbols that arise from the depth requires what Eigen and Bion call "faith in truth," a trusting openness towards the truth of whatever arises in our conversation with the unconscious depth. No symbolic ordering of our lives towards authenticity could take place without faithfully bringing the openness of presence to bear on the symbolic level. We have discovered in symbolic life a correlate of what Fred Lawrence identifies as the "truth-intention" in dialectical conversations. Since it orients the conversants beyond merely self-serving ends, he calls the truth-intention "an immanent principle of self-transcendence." As Lawrence does for the truth-intention, we must admit that faith in truth exercised through conscious presence to symbols appears to originate spontaneously in those who exercise it.

The following diagram (6.1) shows the relation of openness to the symbols arising from the depth to the concurrent exercise of faith in truth. The downward openness to depth would not occur if the upward movement to faith in truth were not also occurring. When we consider this truth-intention of symbolic life, we see that it has no particular object. It does not manipulate reality to conform to any one wish, but enacts a basic openness, come what may; and therein lies its claim to be a "self-transcendent principle." It transcends the limitations of desire for particular objects by opening the subject to whatever symbols arise. It desires the truth that the symbols will mediate.

To put faith in truth, the subject must also ascend to a differentiated state of conscious presence—the still point. Intentional consciousness quite appropriately pursues particular objects as ends. It becomes attached—again, rightly so. The still point, on the other hand, is a consciousness without

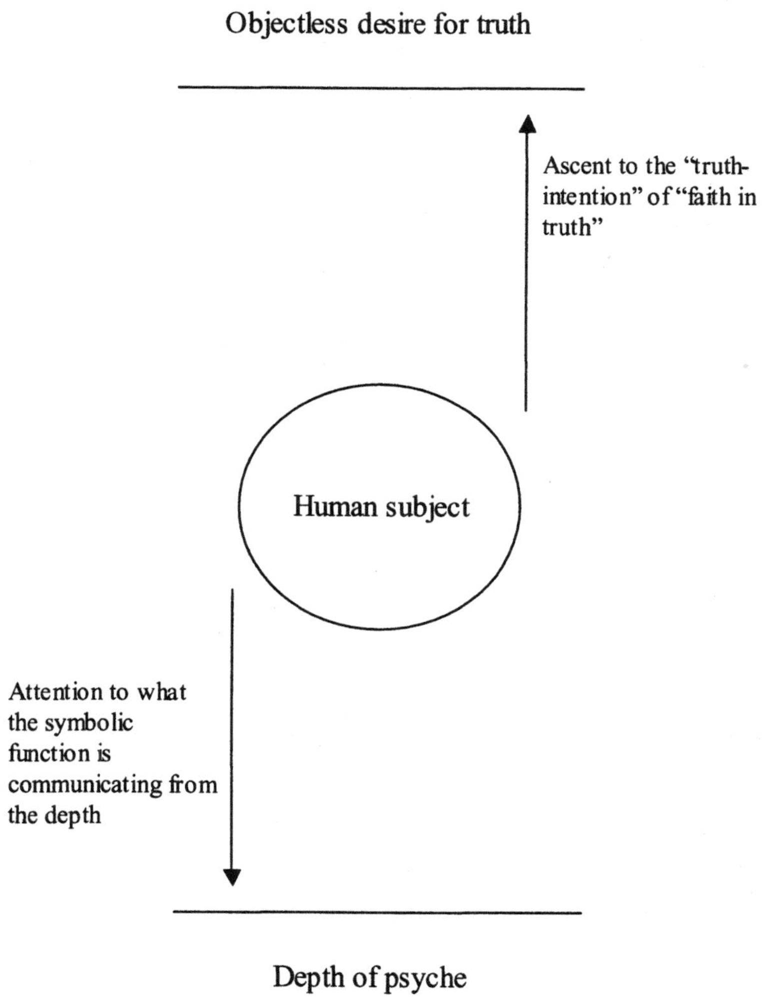
Objectless desire for truth
Ascent to the "truth-intention" of "faith in truth"
Human subject
Attention to what the symbolic function is communicating from the depth
Depth of psyche

Diagram 6.1

contents that allows all contents to exist. It detaches desire from particular objects and concentrates on allowing all things to be just as they are. It desires to bring conscious presence to all things, just as they arise to awareness. Because faith in truth also detaches the subject from particular objects, so that the truth of symbols can make itself known, the subject's ability to put faith in truth benefits from the still point's differentiation. Without ascent to the still point, quite likely the faith in truth would not occur. This I consider the authentic meaning of contemplative detachment—the differentiated nearness of presence. The diagram (6.2) below illustrates my point.

Yet why would we in fact desire the truth? After all, the truths we encounter may prove very unpleasant, even if they do us good. Objectless faith in truth contradicts the suspicious, modern reduction of our natures to pleasure-seeking, pain-avoiding, world-mastering, self-mastering activity. It takes us beyond the realm of purely instinctual desire—mere reflexivity—and even beyond the civilized realm of differentiated desire for good objects. It neglects neither of these, but also transposes us to a state in which desire functions in tandem with contemplative detachment to open our hearts to symbolic truth. At this stage, the mysteries of faith in truth and the still point may engender contemplation of an absolutely transcendent source of these finitely self-transcendent realities. If such contemplation occurs, the subject may identify both the still point and faith in truth as gifts given by this transcendent source—in other words, as the self-revealing of divine grace. My last diagram (6.3) shows this relationship.

Jung's tendency to picture the perfectly individuated person as an independent, invulnerable psychic monad undermines this more salutary direction of his symbolic practice, in which the goal of the developmental process looks very different. If our self-transcendent capacities engender contemplation, the soul will continually reach out beyond itself towards the unknown source of psychic order. Then it will find itself experiencing what Voegelin considers tell-tale signs of the revelation of divine presence—experiences of "seeking, searching, and questioning, of ignorance and knowledge concerning the divine ground, of futility, absurdity, anxiety, and alienation of existence, of being turned around, of return, illumination, and rebirth."[256] Beyond the purely historical question of what Jung thought, we cannot judge whether his view of symbolic life includes openness to divine transcendence solely on the basis of whether his philosophical assumptions allow this openness, or even on whether his phenomenology of symbol

---

[256] *Order and History, v.* 4, 17-18.

formation explicitly mentions it. To make such a judgment, we must first analyze the structure of symbol formation itself. My analysis shows that the openness exists in the symbolic function. By referring to insights from recent psychoanalytic literature, I have been able to present a theology of symbolic life that includes transcendent presence not as a peripheral phenomenon, but as integral to the very structure of the symbolic function.

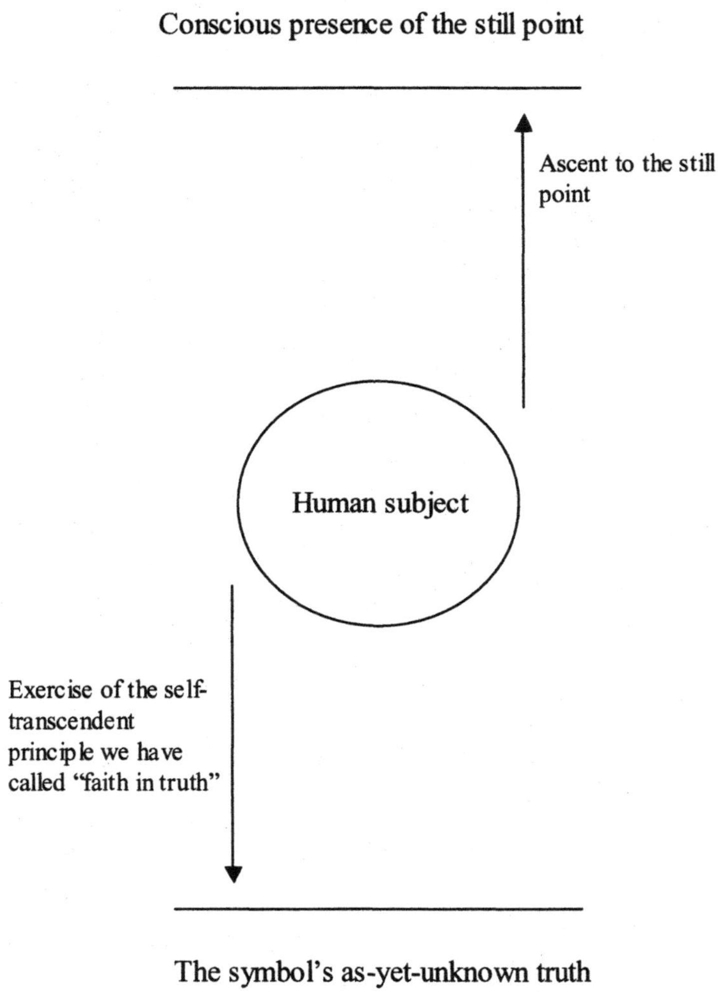
Conscious presence of the still point
Ascent to the still point
Human subject
Exercise of the self-transcendent principle we have called "faith in truth"
The symbol's as-yet-unknown truth

Diagram 6.2

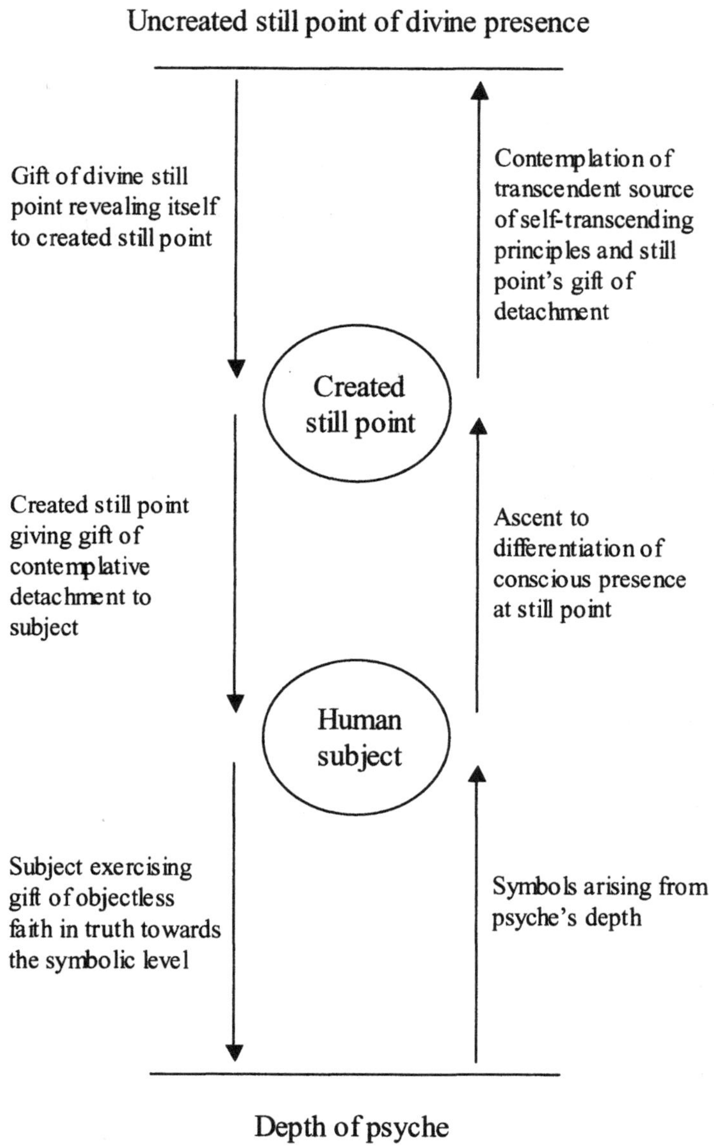
Uncreated still point of divine presence
Gift of divine still point revealing itself to created still point
Contemplation of transcendent source of self-transcending principles and still point's gift of detachment
Created still point
Created still point giving gift of contemplative detachment to subject
Ascent to differentiation of conscious presence at still point
Human subject
Subject exercising gift of objectless faith in truth towards the symbolic level
Symbols arising from psyche's depth
Depth of psyche

Diagram 6.3

Bibliography

Primary Works

N.B. Entire volumes and single essays are listed below the general bibliographic reference for the *Collected Works*, including the title and number of the volume. Other texts which are not part of the *Collected Works* are included alphabetically.

Jung, C. G. *The Collected Works of C.G. Jung* (CW). Ed. Herbert Reed, Michael Fordham, and Gerhard Adler. William McGuire, exec. ed. Bollingen Series XX. Princeton: Princeton University Press, 1953+.

Jung, C.G. *Gesammelte Werke*. Zürich: Rascher, 1958+.

Aion: Researches into the Phenomenology of the Self. CW *9, ii.*

Analytical Psychology: Notes of the Seminar Given in 1925. Ed. William McGuire. Princeton: Princeton University Press, 1991.

"Commentary on *The Secret of the Golden Flower*." In Richard Wilhelm, trans. and ed., *The Secret of the Golden Flower: A Chinese Book of Life*. New York: Harcourt Brace & Company, 1962.

Dream Analysis–Notes of the Seminar Given in 1928-1930. Ed. William McGuire. Princeton: Princeton University Press, 1984.

"Foreword to Suzuki's *Introduction to Zen Buddhism*." *Psychology and Religion: West and East,* CW *11.*

"Individual Dream Symbolism in Relation to Alchemy" (1936). *Psychology and Alchemy.* CW *12.*

Letters: Volume 1: 1906-1950. Selected and ed. Gerhard Adler, in collaboration with Aniela Jaffé. Trans. R. F. C. Hull. Princeton: Princeton University Press, 1973.

Memories, Dreams, Reflections. Ed. Aniela Jaffé. 1961. Trans. Richard and Clara Winston. Revised edition. New York: Vintage Books, 1989.

Nietzsche's Zarathustra: Notes of the Seminar Given in 1934-1939 by C.G. *Jung*. Ed. James L. Jarrett. 2 vols. Princeton: Princeton University Press, 1988.

"On Psychological Understanding" (1914). *The Psychogenesis of Mental Disease.* CW 3.

"Psychological Commentary on *The Tibetan Book of the Great Liberation*." *Psychology and Religion:*

West and East, CW *11*.

Psychological Types (revised). CW *6*.

Psychological Types: Or, The Psychology of Individuation. Trans. H. Godwin Baynes. London: Routledge and Kegan Paul, 1923.

"The Psychology of Eastern Meditation." *Psychology and Religion: West and East*, CW *11*.

The Psychology of Kundalini Yoga: Notes of the Seminar Given in 1932. Ed. Sonu Shamdasani. Princeton: Princeton University Press, 1999.

Psychology of the Unconscious: A Study of the Transformations and Symbolisms of the Libido, A Contribution to the History of the Evolution of Thought. Trans. Beatrice M. Hinkle. 1916. New York: Dodd, Mead, and Company, 1949. This is a translation of *Wandlungen und Symbole der Libido* (1912), which underwent complete revision in 1952 to be translated as CW *5*, *Symbols of Transformation: An Analysis of the Prelude to a Case of Schizophrenia*. I have given preference to the earlier version because of my chosen time frame.

Psychology and Religion: West and East. CW *11*.

"The Role of the Unconscious" (1918). *Civilization in Transition*. CW *10*.

"The Structure of the Psyche" (1927/1931). *The Structure and Dynamics of the Psyche*. CW *8*.

"A Study in the Process of Individuation" (1934/1950). *Archetypes and the Collective Unconscious*. CW *9, i*.

The Symbolic Life: Miscellaneous Writings. CW *18*.

"The Tavistock Lectures" (1935). *The Symbolic Life: Miscellaneous Writings*, CW *18*.

"The Transcendent Function" ([1916]/1957). *The Structure and Dynamics of the Psyche*. CW *8*.

Two Essays on Analytical Psychology. CW *7*.

Visions: Notes of the Seminar Given in 1930-1934. Ed. Claire Douglas. 2 vols. Princeton: Princeton University Press, 1997.

"Yoga and the West." *Psychology and Religion: West and East*, CW *11*.

The Zofingia Lectures. Supplementary Volume A to the *Collected Works*. Ed. William McGuire. Trans. Jan van Heurck, 1983.

Secondary Works

Adler, Gerhard. *The Living Symbol: A Case Study in the Process of Individuation*. New York, Pantheon Books, 1961.

Altizer, Thomas J. J. "A Critical Analysis of C.G. Jung's Understanding of Religion." Ph.D. Dissertation. University of Chicago, 1955.

Bair, Deirdre. *Jung: A Biography*. Boston: Little, Brown and Company. 2003.

Barz, Helmut, Verena Kast, and Frank Nager. *Heilung und Wandlung: C.G. Jung und die Medizin*. Zürich: Artemis Verlag, 1986.

Bion, Wilfred R. *Seven Servants: Four Works*. New York: Jason Aronson, 1977.

Bollas, Christopher. *Cracking Up: The Work of Unconscious Experience*. New York: Hill and Wang, 1995.

——. *The Mystery of Things*. New York: Routledge, 1999.

——. *The Shadow of the Object: Psychoanalysis of the Unthought Known*. New York: Columbia

University Press, 1987.

Brooke, Roger. *Pathways into the Jungian World: Phenomenology and Analytical Psychology*. New York: Routledge, 1999.

Brooke, Roger. "Analytical Psychology and Existential Phenomenology: An Integration and a Clinical Study." *The Psychoanalytic Review* 83(4): 525-545.

Brooks, Henry Curtis. "Analytical Psychology and the Image of God." *Andover Newton Quarterly* 6, November 1965: 35-55.

Brown, Anne. "Language and the Emerging Symbol." *Journal of Analytical Psychology* 33(3), July 1988: 277-297.

Brown, Clifford A. *Jung's Hermeneutic of Doctrine: Its Theological Significance*. Chico, CA: Scholars Press, 1981.

Campbell, Joseph. "The Symbol without Meaning." Photocopy from *Eranos Jahrbuch*, v. 26, 1957: 415-475.

Charet, F.X. *Spiritualism and the Foundations of C.G. Jung's Psychology*. Albany: State University of New York Press, 1993.

Clarke, J.J. *In Search of Jung: Historical and Philosophical Enquiries*. New York: Routledge, 1992.

Clift, Wallace B. *Jung and Christianity: The Challenge of Reconciliation*. New York: Crossroad, 1982.

Corbett Lionel. "A Depth Psychological Approach to the Sacred." In *Depth Psychology: Meditations in the Field*. Ed. Dennis Slattery and Lionel Corbett. Einsiedeln, Switzerland: Daimon, 2000

——. *The Religious Function of the Psyche*. New York: Routledge, 1996.

Doran, Robert. "Jung and Catholic Theology," in *Catholicism and Jungian Psychology*. Ed. J. Marvin Spiegelman. Phoenix, AZ: Falcon Press, 1988.

Dourley, John P. C.G. *Jung and Paul Tillich: The Psyche as Sacrament*. Toronto: Inner City Books, 1981.

——. *The Illness That We Are: A Jungian Critique of Christianity*. Toronto: Inner City Books, 1984.

——. "The Innate Capacity: Jung and the Mystical Imperative." *The Innate Capacity: Mysticism, Psychology, and Philosophy*. Ed. Robert K.C. Forman. New York: Oxford University Press, 1998.

——. *A Strategy for a Loss of Faith: Jung's Proposal*. Toronto: Inner City Books, 1992.

Edinger, Edward F. *Creation of Consciousness: Jung's Myth for Modern Man*. Toronto, Inner City Books, 1995.

——. *Ego and Archetype: Individuation and the Religious Function of the Psyche*. Boston: Shambhala, 1992.

——. *The New God-Image: A Study of Jung's Key Letters Concerning the Evolution of the Western God-Image*. Wilmette, IL: Chiron Publications, 1996.

Eigen, Michael. "The Area of Faith in Winnicott, Lacan and Bion." In *Relational Psychoanalysis: The Emergence of a Tradition*. Ed. Stephen Mitchell and Lewis Aron. Hillsdale, NJ: The Analytic Press, 1999.

——. *The Psychoanalytic Mystic*. New York: Free Association Books, 1998.

Ellenberger, Henri F. *The Discovery of the Unconscious: The History and Evolution of Dynamic Psychiatry*. New York: Basic Books, 1970.

Ellman, Carolyn S., Stanley Grand, Mark Silvan, and Steven J. Ellman (eds.). *The Modern*

Freudians: Contemporary Psychoanalytic Technique. Northvale, NJ: Jason Aronson, 1998.

Flanagan, Joseph. *Quest for Self-Knowledge: An Essay in Lonergan's Philosophy*. Toronto: University of Toronto Press, 1997.

Fordham, Michael. "Reflections on Image and Symbol." *Journal of Analytical Psychology*, v. 2, January 1957: 85-92.

——. "The Emergence of a Symbol in a Five-year-old Child." *Journal of Analytical Psychology*, v. 5, 1960: 33-40.

Forsyth, James. *Freud, Jung, and Christianity*. Ottawa: University of Ottawa Press, 1989.

Frey-Rohn, Liliane. *From Freud to Jung: A Comparative Study of the Psychology of the Unconscious*. Trans. Fred E. Engreen and Evelyn K. Engreen. Boston: Shambhala, 1990.

Grotstein, James. "The numinous and immanent nature of the psychoanalytic Subject." *Journal of Analytical Psychology* 43 (1998): 41-68.

——. *Who is the Dreamer Who Dreams the Dream? A Study of Psychic Presences*. Hillsdale, NJ: The Analytic Press, 2000.

Hanna, Charles Bartruff. *The Face of the Deep: The Religious Ideas of C.G. Jung*. Philadelphia: Westminster Press, 1967.

Harding, M. Esther. *Psychic Energy: Its Source and Its Transformation*. Second Edition. Princeton: Princeton University Press, 1963.

——. "Jung's Contribution to Religious Symbolism." *Spring*. 1959: 1-16.

Hayman, Ronald. *A Life of Jung*. New York: W.W. Norton & Company, 1999.

Heisig, James W. *Imago Dei: A Study of C.G. Jung's Psychology of Religion*. Lewisburg: Bucknell University Press, 1979.

Henderson, Joseph Lewis. "Transcendence: Symbols of Man's Search for Self." *Psychological Perspectives* 1(1) Spring 1970: 34-42.

Hillman, James. *Insearch: Psychology and Religion*. Second Edition. Woodstock, CT: Spring Publications, 1996.

——. *Re-Visioning Psychology*. New York: Harper Perennial, 1976.

Homans, Peter. *Jung in Context: Modernity and the Making of a Psychology*. Second Edition. Chicago: University of Chicago Press, 1995.

Hostie, Raymond. *Religion and the Psychology of Jung*. New York: Sheed & Ward, 1957.

Hughes, Glenn. *Mystery and Myth in the Philosophy of Eric Voegelin*. Columbia: University of Missouri Press, 1993.

—— (ed.). *The Politics of the Soul: Eric Voegelin on Religious Experience*. New York: Rowman and Littlefield, 1999.

Jacobi, Jolande. *Complex/Archetype/Symbol in the Psychology of C.G. Jung*. Trans. Ralph Manheim. Bollingen Series LVII. Princeton: Princeton University Press, 1959.

——. *The Psychology of C. G. Jung: An Introduction with Illustrations*, with a Foreword by Dr. Jung. Trans. Ralph Manheim. New Haven: Yale University Press, 1973.

Kaufmann, Walter Arnold. *Discovering the Mind: Volume Three, Freud versus Adler and Jung*. New York: McGraw-Hill, 1980.

Kelly, Sean M. *Individuation and the Absolute: Hegel, Jung, and the Path toward Wholeness*. New York: Paulist Press, 1993.

Kerr, John. *A Most Dangerous Method: The Story of Jung, Freud, and Sabina Speilrein*. New York:

Alfred A. Knopf, 1993.

Lammers, Ann Conrad. *In God's Shadow: The Collaboration of Victor White and C.G. Jung*. New York: Paulist Press, 1994.

Lawrence, Frederick. "Language as Horizon." In *The Beginning and the Beyond: Papers from the Gadamer and Voegelin Conferences*, Supplementary Issue of Lonergan Workshop, Volume 4, Edited by Frederick Lawrence, 13-34. Chico: Scholar's Press, 1984.

Mattoon, Mary Ann. *Jungian Psychology in Perspective*. New York: The Free Press, 1981.

Mattoon, Mary Ann (ed.). *The Transcendent Function: Individual and Collective Aspects*. Einsiedeln, Switzerland: Diamon Verlag, 1993.

McDargh, John. *Psychoanalytic Object Relations Theory and the Study of Religion: On Faith and the Imaging of God*. Lanham, MD: University Press, 1983.

Meier, C. A. Jung's *Analytical Psychology and Religion*. Carbondale: Southern Illinois University Press, 1977.

Mitchell, Stephen A., and Lewis Aron (eds.). *Relational Psychoanalysis: The Emergence of a Tradition*. Hillsdale, NJ: The Analytic Press, 1999.

Mitchell, Stephen A., and Margaret J. Black (eds.). *Freud and Beyond: A History of Modern Psychoanalytic Thought*. New York: BasicBooks, 1995.

Moore, Robert L. and Daniel J. Mechel, eds. *Jung and Christianity in Dialogue: Faith, Feminism, and Hermeneutics*. New York: Paulist Press, 1990.

Moore, Robert L. "Ritual Process, Initiation, and Contemporary Religion." In *Jung's Challenge to Contemporary Religion*. Ed. Murray Stein and Robert L. Moore. Wilmette, IL: Chiron Publications, 1987.

Moreno, Antonio. *Jung, Gods, & Modern Man*. Notre Dame: University of Notre Dame Press, 1970.

Morrissey, Michael. *Consciousness and Transcendence: The Theology of Eric Voegelin*. Notre Dame: University of Notre Dame Press, 1994.

Nagy, Marilyn. "Jung and Kaufmann: The Father Complex." *Psychological Perspectives* 14(1) (1983): 111-122.

Nagy, Marilyn. *Philosophical Issues in the Psychology of C.G. Jung*. Albany: State University of New York Press, 1991.

Noll, Richard. *The Jung Cult: Origins of a Charismatic Movement*. Princeton: Princeton University Press, 1994.

Ogden, Thomas. *Conversations at the Frontier of Dreaming*. Northvale, NJ: Jason Aronson, 2001.

——. "Potential Space." In *The Matrix of the Mind: Object Relations and the Psychoanalytic Dialogue*. Northvale, NJ: Jason Aronson, 1993.

——. *Subjects of Analysis*. Northvale, NJ: Jason Aronson, 1994.

Otto, Rudolf. *The Idea of the Holy*. Second edition. Oxford: Oxford University Press, 1950.

Palmer, Michael. *Freud and Jung on Religion*. New York: Routledge, 1997.

Rieff, Philip. *Freud: The Mind of the Moralist*. Third edition. Chicago: University of Chicago Press, 1979.

——. *The Triumph of the Therapeutic: Uses of Faith after Freud*. Chicago: University of Chicago Press, 1987.

Ryce-Menuhin, Joel. *Jung and the Monotheisms: Judaism, Christianity, and Islam*. New York: Routledge, 1994.

Rychlak, Joseph F. "Jung as Dialectician and Teleologist." In *Jung in Modern Perspective*. Ed. Renos K. Papadopoulos and Graham S. Saayman. Hounslow, Middlesex: Wildwood House, 1984.

Samuels, Andrew. *Jung and the Post-Jungians*. New York: Routledge, 1985.

Schwabe, Julius. *Archetyp und Tierkreis: Grundlinien einer Kosmischen Symbolik und Mythologie*. Basel: Beno Schwabe, 1951.

Shamdasani, Sonu. *Cult Fictions: C.G. Jung and the Founding of Analytical Psychology*. New York: Routledge, 1998.

——. *Jung and the Making of Modern Psychology: The Dream of a Science*. Cambridge: Cambridge University Press, 2003.

Singer, June. *Seeing through the Visible World: Jung, Gnosis, and Chaos*. San Francisco: Harper & Row, 1990.

Spiegel, David, ed. *Dissociation: Culture, Mind, and Body*. Washington, D.C.: American Psychiatric Press, 1994.

Stein, Leopold. "What is a Symbol Supposed to Be?" *Journal of Analytical Psychology*, v. 2, January 1957: 73-84.

Stein, Murray. "Jung's Green Christ: A Healing Symbol for Christianity." In *Jung's Challenge to Contemporary Religion*. Ed. Murray Stein and Robert L. Moore. Wilmette, IL: Chiron Publications, 1987.

——. *Jung's Treatment of Christianity: The Psychotherapy of a Religious Tradition*. Wilmette, IL: Chiron Publications, 1985.

——. *Practicing Wholeness: Analytical Psychology and Jungian Thought*. New York: Continuum, 1996.

Stephens, Barbara D. "The Martin Buber-Carl Jung Disputations: Protecting the Sacred in the Battle for the Boundaries of Analytical Psychology." *Journal of Analytical Psychology* 46 (2001): 455-91

——. "The Return of the Prodigal: The Emergence of Jungian Themes in Post-Freudian Thought." *Journal of Analytical Psychology* 44 (1999): 197-220.

Sulloway, Frank J. *Freud, Biologist of the Mind: Beyond the Psychoanalytic Legend*. New York: Basic Books, 1979.

Taylor, Eugene. "The New Jung Scholarship." *Psychoanalytic Review* 83(4) August 1996: 547-568.

——. *Shadow Culture: Psychology and Spirituality in America*. Washington, D.C.: Counterpoint, 1999.

Tenzler, Johannes. *Selbstfindung und Gotteserfahrung*. München: Verlag Ferdinand Schöningh, 1975.

Tresan, David I. "Response to Buber/Jung Paper." Obtained through personal correspondence with the author (to be published in the July 2002 issue of the *Journal of Analytical Psychology*).

Ulanov, Ann Belford. *The Functioning Transcendent: A Study in Analytical Psychology*. Wilmette, IL: Chiron Publications, 1996.

Ulanov, Ann Belford, and Barry Ulanov. *Religion and the Unconscious*. Philadelphia: The Westminster Press, 1975.

Voegelin, Eric. "The Beginning and the Beyond: A Meditation on Truth." In *What is History? And Other Late Unpublished Writings*, v. 28 in *The Collected Works of Eric Voegelin*. Ed.

Thomas A. Hollweck and Paul Caringella. Baton Rouge: Louisiana State University Press, 1990.

——. *Order and History*, v. 4, *The Ecumenic Age*. Baton Rouge: LSU Press, 1974.

——. *Order and History*, v. 5, *In Search of Order*. Ed. Ellis Sandoz. Columbia: University of Missouri Press, 2000.

——. "The Political Religions." In *Modernity without Restraint*. Ed. Manfred Henningsen. *The Collected Works of Eric Voegelin*, v. 5. Columbia: University of Missouri Press, 2000.

von Franz, Marie-Louise. *Spiegelungen der Seele: Projektion und innere Sammlung in der Psychologie* C.G. *Jungs*. Stuttgart: Kreuz Verlag, 1978.

Wehr, Gerhard. *Jung: A Biography*. Trans. David M. Weeks. Shambhala: Boston, 1987.

Whitmont, Edward C. "Nature, Symbol, and Imaginal Reality." Spring. 1971: 64-83.

Index

FSC
www.fsc.org
MIX
Papier | Fördert gute Waldnutzung
FSC® C083411

Kolibri 360 GmbH
Ferdinand-Jühlke-Straße 7
99095 Erfurt, Deutschland
produktsicherheit@kolibri360.de

Druck:
CPI Druckdienstleistungen GmbH
im Auftrag der
Kolibri 360 GmbH
Ferdinand-Jühlke-Str. 7
99095 Erfurt